IMAGES
of America

AFRICAN-AMERICAN
ENTERTAINMENT IN
ATLANTA

This is a collage of entertainers who graced the night clubs and stages of Atlanta's African-American venues during the 1960s. (Reprinted from the *Atlanta Daily World*.)

Cover image: Ma Rainey and her Georgia Band (*c.* 1920) were regular performers at the 81 Theater on Decatur Street.

IMAGES
of America

AFRICAN-AMERICAN
ENTERTAINMENT IN
ATLANTA

Herman "Skip" Mason, Jr.

ARCADIA

Published by Arcadia Publishing,
an imprint of Tempus Publishing, Inc.
2 Cumberland Street
Charleston, SC 29401

Printed in Great Britain.

Library of Congress Catalog Card Number: 98-85875

For all general information contact Arcadia Publishing at:
Telephone 843-853-2070
Fax 843-853-0044
E-Mail arcadia@charleston.net

For customer service and orders:
Toll-Free 1-888-313-BOOK

Visit us on the internet at http://www.arcadiaimages.com

To Mama, for taking me to my first James Brown concert in 1969; to "Pop," for your support; to the memory of my beloved band director at Morris Brown College, Cleopas "Prof." Johnson; to Clarence Hubbard, whose efforts to document the musicians in the 1960s made it possible for me to complete this publication; to the late Jondelle Johnson; to Harmon Perry, for your gift of photography; to the Atlanta Daily World newspaper, undeniably the most important resource for documenting the rich history of African Americans in Atlanta; and to "Youngblood," for keeping the music of yesteryear alive in our memories.

This is a night at the YMCA Canteen with the Stardusters Band providing the music, c. 1950.

Contents

Music has always been an important form of entertainment for African-American families. Following Emancipation, rural families began to migrate to Atlanta, bringing their musical talents with them. (Courtesy of the Library of Congress.)

Introduction

This publication, *African-American Entertainment in Atlanta*, documents through pictures and text some of the individuals and institutions which comprised the entertainment industry in Atlanta from post–Civil War to the 1970s. This is not meant to be the definitive study but just a glimpse at a very rich past. The book looks at the dance halls, night clubs, musicians, managers, promoters, and local performers in the African-American community in Atlanta, as well as those entertainers who brought their talent to the stages of Atlanta through many never-before-published images from the Digging It Up Archives. Omitted from this volume are the theaters and movie houses which African Americans patronized. The information researched and collected on that subject is extensive and is deserving of its own volume. Nevertheless, in addition to the night spots, this publication recalls the various forms of music which characterize the numerous decades covered that helped to set a time frame for the diversity of music forms as they were introduced to the Atlanta community. This includes minstrel, ragtime, vaudeville, blues, jazz, classical, rhythm and blues, and soul.

African-American Entertainment in Atlanta focuses on the local performers in Atlanta such as the Whitman Sisters, Little Richard (a Macon transplant), James Brown (an Augusta transplant), Chuck "the Sheik" Willis, Gladys Knight and the Pips, Thomas Dorsey, Big Maybelle, and many others who later went on to gain national prominence and whose crafts were developed in local establishments in the city.

As a child, I remember very vividly one Saturday evening, when my mother (then pregnant with my sister) and I headed down to the old City Auditorium to see James Brown and his revue. The year was 1969 and I was seven years old. I recall sitting on the floor of the auditorium in folding chairs and then when Brown began to perform seeing the chairs fold up with the voracity of electricity as he ranted, and did his famous theatrical routine for his song, "Please, Please, Please."

I also remember listening to my mother and father talk about some of the dances at the Lincoln Country Club and the shows that they went to see at the Royal Peacock and the Palladium, where they enjoyed the entertainment of such greats as Aretha Franklin, Sam Cooke, and Marvin Gaye (who, according to her, had a blue velvet suit). Her experiences were documented at the club thanks to photographers such as Count Jackson and others who would go from table to table photographing the guests. One photograph shows my mother and step-father enjoying a night at the Royal Peacock along with other relatives and singer Jackie Moore, who had a hit in the 1960s called "Precious, Precious." Later I would discover that for over 75 years, hundreds, perhaps thousands of African Americans in Atlanta reveled and relished in the most exciting entertainment city south of the Mason-Dixon Line. Yes, Memphis had its Beale Street and the blues lingered on, but entertainment in Atlanta was different. And those who entertained and those who were being entertained knew it.

Even in the first 100-year history of the city, there was something magnetic about Atlanta and the people it attracted, and entertainment crossed class lines within the black community. Before Sweet Auburn's heyday, the upper-class considered it "criminal" to be caught dead on Decatur Street, where African-American night life thrived as colorful and rich as any Chester Himes's novel.

But as history will record, the social classes met head-to-head on Auburn Avenue, and the outcome was powerful. The bottom line was that good music was played, dancers danced, comedians created laughter, and African Americans, though denied of many constitutional rights and being prohibited from mixing in the mainstream of society because of their color, could shake, rattle, and roll because entertainment knew no sex, color, or creed. In 1961, at an all-white dinner party hosted by then-mayor William B. Hartsfield, Hank Ballard, who was the originator of the dance craze "the Twist," performed for hours at the Dinkler Hotel Garden. Hartsfield exclaimed, "Ballard and his Midnighters launched the dance in Georgia in 1958. This is the greatest Twist party ever." While in my office at the Atlanta Fulton Public Library in the late 1980s, I came across a file with a wealth of material on African-American businessman, educator, and entertainment promoter J. Neal Montgomery. By the time I finished going through the collection, I could only imagine what Atlanta must have been like during 1930s and 1940s , when nationally known entertainers pulled into town to give its fans and patrons the best entertainment for their money.

Several years ago, I attended a dinner dance for a very well-noted and respected group in Atlanta. As in the past, the organization featured a nationally known entertainer. This particular year the singer was Gladys Knight. During her opening number, she began to recall some of the night spots of the fifties and sixties, and there was a collective voice of approval from those who were old enough to remember the places. However, many in the audience were not natives of Atlanta and those places did not really have any meaning to them. It was at that point that I knew that this book had to be done and soon. When I read a *Billboard* article labeling Atlanta as the new "Motown," it was clear that a publication on the history of entertainment in Atlanta was mandatory and that there were many stories to be told.

African-American Entertainment in Atlanta is an area of history of which very little has been documented. Though Harlem may have been the site of the cultural renaissance of the North, it can be clearly stated that Atlanta was the home of the African-American renaissance in the South following the race riot of 1906 to the 1930s. Virtually every known entertainer and musician in the country appeared in Atlanta. These entertainers traveled the "chittling circuit" and came to Atlanta on broken-down buses and down segregated back roads to perform on its stages. For W.C. Handy, Bessie Smith, Ma Rainey, Duke Ellington, Count Basie, the Nicholas Brothers, Ella Fitzgerald, Sarah Vaughan, Jackie Wilson, Dinah Washington, the Motown Revue, and even the legendary Billie Holiday and hundreds of others, Atlanta's club scene was a must stop. They resided at the Savoy Hotel, the Royal Hotel, the Forrest Arms (managed by

Ms. Johnnie Jefferson) on Butler Street, and later Paschal's Hotel, before desegregation opened the fine hotels downtown.

During the annual Sweet Auburn Festival in 1991, I had the opportunity to attend a black-tie affair at the Royal Peacock. I imagined what it must have been like in the late 1940s, 1950s, and 1960s to get ready for a show at the Peacock on Sweet Auburn. The street was lit up with neon lights beaming from the Savoy Hotel in the Herndon Building, and the words "Jesus Saves" in blue neon lights illuminated from the steeple of Big Bethel A.M.E. Church. As I climbed up the steps of the Peacock, I imagined the thousands of patrons who had ascended the stairs to Atlanta's Club Beautiful. Though much larger inside, the club was everything I had imagined. As I approached my seat near the stage, I began to think about the hundreds of musicians who performed on it. I thought about the Top Hat Floorshows of the 1940s and also the fabulous fraternity dances and parties held there.

That night the guest performer was Arthur Prysock, who had performed at the Peacock in the 1950s and 1960s. The master of ceremonies was none other than James "Alley Pat" Patrick, a radio disc jockey with a raunchy mouth who had introduced hundreds of stars. The other special guest was Jack "the Rapper" Gibson, who also worked at WERD radio station and was known as Jockey Jack Gibson, now the creator of the Family Affair Convention, one of the largest gathering of radio and record moguls, new entertainers, and prominent record producers. The "Jack the Rapper" Convention was a phenomenal event. The blaring of the band and the carnival atmosphere further confirmed my desire to write this book.

A visit to the Fala Hen Dress Show on Auburn Avenue served as a divine intervention. The owner of the dress shop was the granddaughter of Irvin Favors, the owner of the famous Club Zanzibar and the Auburn Avenue Casino lobby of the Auburn Avenue Casino. I convinced her to show me the club. After locating the key and stepping through the club's door, I also stepped back in time. The facility was huge, filled with tables, chairs, and other items that had been frozen in time. I walked to the stage to get a feel of what one of the entertainers might have seen on the Casino stage. Of course, I searched for any and all artifacts and was lucky to find an Auburn Avenue Casino poster, a program book and ticket for a Jackie Wilson concert, and a picture of the Bronner Brothers Hair Convention held at the Casino. I later learned that the large halls in Atlanta, such as the Magnolia Ballroom and the Auburn Casino, were the convention sites and meeting places for African American in the fifties and sixties before the downtown hotels opened their doors to African Americans.

Today as I drive through Atlanta, there are virtually no remnants of the old Decatur Street and the 81 Theater, as well as the other Bailey Theaters—with exception of the old Ashby Street Theater, which is now used as a church. Clubs like the Magnolia Ballroom and the Lincoln Country Club are now leveled to the ground. With integration, many of the downtown clubs became sparsely attended. Police raids during the 1960s were abundant. In one night alone in 1960, 100 people were arrested on such charges as gaming, occupying a dive, and drunkenness. By the 1970s, other clubs had replaced the old line clubs including Club Atlantis at the Hyatt Regency, Club Aquarius, the Apothecary, the Colonial Club, Cadillac Lounge, the Playboy Club, the Pendulum Club, the Gold Lounge, and the Living Room Lounge. Musicians and singers had the opportunity to play other larger venues such as the Omni and the City Auditorium. The intimacy of the small clubs was gone. But the spirit and excitement of the entertainers, the music that permeated the air, the neon club lights, and a night on the "Avenue" or one of the other "joints" linger within the minds and in the memories of all those fortunate Atlantans who "shook, rattled, and rolled" during a phenomenal period in Atlanta's history. The nineties have given us Don Rivers Productions, LaFace Records, Club Eschelon, Mr. V's, Jazzmin's, and large venues such as the Fox, the Civic Center, Chastain and Lakewood Amphitheaters, and numerous other venues throughout the city. It is hoped that this publication will recapture in a very small way those unfamiliar, long-forgotten faces and names of a rich bygone era in the history of Atlanta whose story has not been told until now.

—SM

One
The Early History

During and after slavery, African Americans realized the necessity to keep themselves entertained musically. Young males primarily learned how to play such instruments as the fiddle and the guitar. The earliest known entertainer to perform in Atlanta at the Athenaeum Theater, Atlanta's only antebellum theater, was Tom Bethune, a blind, self-taught musician from a south Georgia plantation. He first appeared in Atlanta in 1857 and later appeared five times during the 1860s. In one concert, he played simultaneously "Dixie" with one hand and "Yankee Doodle" with the other, while singing "The Girl I Left Behind Me."

From the 1880s to the early 1900s, African Americans in Atlanta were entertained by traveling minstrel companies and local orchestras which performed at social events held at the first Odd Fellows Hall, located on Piedmont Avenue. Atlanta University offered musically talented students, including James Weldon Johnson, brother of J. Rosamond Johnson, who entertained throughout the city during the late 1890s. (Reprinted from *The Black Side*.)

Numerous churches in Atlanta held annual concerts allowing performing artists a venue to sing and play to their own race. The African-American community in Atlanta looked forward with great anticipation to its Colored Music Festival, during which some of the finest talent in the world was brought to the city. This included Harry T. Burleigh, Madam Anita Patti Brown, the Fisk Jubilee Singers, violinist Joseph Douglas (son of Frederick Douglas), and others.

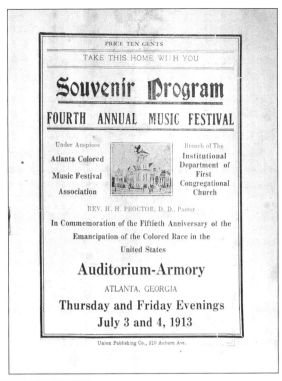

Madame Anita Patti Brown, a coloratura from Chicago, was one of many artists who came to Atlanta, performing at First Congregational Church. When she performed at the Odd Fellows Auditorium Theater on December 5, 1916, general admission was 35¢ and reserved seats were 65¢. (Courtesy of Charles and Amaryllis Hawk.)

Between 1910 and 1915, the Odd Fellows Building and Auditorium provided a venue for dances on its "Roof Garden" and gave African Americans an opportunity to see first-class performances such as "Black Patti" and her Troubadours, Salem Tutt Whitney, and the Whitman Sisters in its own auditorium/theater, rather than attending one of the numerous Jim Crow theaters in Atlanta. In 1913, the Order of the Odd Fellows completed the construction of the tallest building in Atlanta owned by African Americans, a facility that featured a sixth-floor dance hall (seen here). The building was designed by a young African American and constructed by Robert Edward Pharrow. Pharrow, a native of Washington, Georgia, had constructed buildings on the campus of Morehouse College, as well as in Alabama and other places in Georgia. (Courtesy of the Atlanta History Center.)

THE CRISIS

Vol. 8—No. 1　　　　MAY, 1914　　　　Whole No. 43

In 1914, two years after the opening of the Odd Fellows Building (shown on the cover of the *Crisis* magazine in 1914), the Roof Garden facility opened. It was a large, open ballroom on the sixth floor of the building. The Roof Garden committee, which included such prominent African Americans as Harry H. Pace, Jackson McHenry, and Henry Lincoln Johnson, made it very clear what their expectations were. In a newspaper advertisement announcing the opening, it was stated that "the garden was not built for a dance hall as it has been advertised. The place will be dedicated for meetings . . . concerts, musicals, conventions, meetings, secular and religious, and athletic and college sports."

Advertisements such as this one appeared in the *Atlanta Independent* newspaper until it ceased publication in 1927.

AUDITORIUM ARMORY HALL
Saturday, MATINEE And NITE FEB. 12

Prices—75c, $1, $1.50, $2

MAMIE SMITH
——And Her Original——
JAZZ HOUNDS
Supported by a Company of 18 Colored Artists

Greatest Colored Singer
— OF —
BLUES
in the World

—SEATS ON SALE AT—
Jas. K. Polk Furniture Co.,
288 Decatur Street.
Atlanta Phonograph Company,
18 North Pryor Street.
Kenny Furniture Company,
246 Peters Street.

MAMIE
SMITH

Sings only for OKeh Records. She is the greatest singer of blues in the world.

Hear her Records, then hear this concert.

SHE SINGS—
"Crazy Blues"
"Mem'ries of Mammy"
"It's Right Here For You"
"The Road Is Rocky"
"Fare Thee Honey Blues"
"That Thing Called Love"

From the 1910s to the late 1960s, Bailey's 81 Theater on Decatur Street, considered to be a red light district, was a breeding ground for young African-American musicians and dancers in Atlanta. For Atlanta, this theater was the Lafayette and later Apollo Theaters of the South. It was where Noble Sissle and Eubie Blake brought their sensational Broadway musical *Shuffle Along* for Atlanta audiences to view. Though the 81 catered to black audiences, there were special nights reserved for whites. Colonel Bailey also added movie houses to his chain of theaters for African Americans, like the Royal, Lincoln, Strand, Ashby, Carver, and Harlem Theaters, which showed popular movies of the time.

Atlanta's Jim Crow theaters welcomed African-American patrons as long as they knew where to sit. It was at the 81 Theater where black vaudevillians, both locally and nationally known, would perform on its stage complete with a pit orchestra. Even before "talking movies" became the rage, African Americans could witness surely what was a marvel in technology as these movies were shown, preceded or followed by a stage show, which usually went late into the night and the early morning.

Many of the entertainers who had performed at the 81 were also creating records, and Atlanta became the site of three temporary recording laboratories, including Columbia, Paramount, and Okeh Records. This was done to expand their roster of artists to meet the demands of the growing market for race music. These companies sent talent scouts and announcements to local music stores and relied heavily upon newspapers such as the *Atlanta Independent* to attract new talent. Shown above are Ma Rainey and her Georgia band, featuring Al Wynn on trombone, Dave Nelson on trumpet, and Tom Dorsey on piano.

Tom Dorsey, prolific and gifted musician of the Big Band era, was born in Villa Ricca, Georgia.

One of the most talented of the 1920s blues musician was Willie Samuel McTell, known as "Blind Willie." Born in Thomson, Georgia, in 1901, he ran away from home to tour with carnivals, minstrels, and medicine shows in his early teens. He developed his craft by playing a 12-string guitar and was influenced musically by bluesmen Lonnie Johnson and Blind Willie Johnson. By 1927, McTell recorded with the Victor Label in Atlanta and later Okeh. Blind Willie could often be seen on the streets of Atlanta, especially Decatur Street, where he worked at the 81 Theater. He traveled throughout the North in the 1930s, performing in Chicago and making more recordings for other record labels.

By the late 1930s, African Americans in Atlanta sought to meet their entertainment needs at a variety of nightclubs and dance halls. During the 1920s and before, public dance halls were limited and often dances and parties were held in private homes. Such was the case on Ashby Street where two sisters (one known as Mrs. Smith) who resided at 28 Ashby Street allowed their homes to be used for small dances. Just a few blocks north, the Cannon Home (seen here), later Hanley's Ashby Street Funeral Home, also opened its doors for small dances and parties. Even the Lady of Lourdes Catholic School on Boulevard (near Auburn Avenue) had a dance hall facility.

Something New

ATLANTA IS GOING TO HAVE A NEW BAND

The TOP HATTERS

PLAYING A

DANCE TONITE

FROM 9:30 'TIL 1:30

COVER CHARGE 25c

TOP HAT

According to reports in the *Atlanta Daily World*, the opening of the Top Hat Club was spectacular. The club opened up with a black-tie affair and a maximum capacity of 1,000 people in attendance. Joe Lawrence was a well-known show-business veteran who helped open the Top Hat Club and produced its first show. He also created the show, *Lunch Call*, at radio station WERD.

Many of the bands that played the Top Hat were home grown, including the house band, known as the Top Hatters. The bands would perform at the Midnight Proms, which took place from 12:01 a.m. to the wee hours of the morning.

The Club Beautiful
ATLANTA, GEORGIA

The opening of the Top Hat Club at 186 Auburn Avenue was one of the most highly anticipated events in Atlanta. When it opened on Wednesday, May 5, 1937, it was billed as "the South's Smartest Ballroom." Later it would be known as Atlanta's Club Beautiful. Lorimer Milton, Jesse B. Blayton, and Clayton R. Yates, three young, industrious African-American businessmen, purchased the building on Auburn Avenue. They had formed a corporation known as BLYMIYA. Yates and Milton owned a chain of drugstores and Blayton owned an accounting firm. Blayton was one of the early African Americans in Atlanta to become a certified public accountant. T. Shelton Coles, who had befriended J.B. Blayton, suggested to him that the upstairs space become a nightclub.

The opening guest band was Andy Kirk (seen here) and his Twelve Clouds of Joy. The following night, dubbed an "All Southern Night," featured the Bama State Revelers Band and local celebrity Gladys La Pallmore. The Top Hat was opened from Monday through Friday for African Americans and Saturday nights for whites, who were known to pack the club on their special night. (Courtesy of Digging It Up Archives.)

1940 EDITION OF THE
WHITMAN SISTERS
Starring
POPS and LOUIE
"America's Greatest Dance Team"
(Direct from their European Triumph)
ALICE AND BERT
"America's Sweethearts of Rhythm"
MISS PRISCILLA ROYSTER
"Detroit's Gift to Swing"
Original Harlem Lindy Hoppers
"Jitterbugs at Their Best"
JOHNNY (Skat) TAYLOR   **MATTHEW RUCKER**
Nationaly Known Skat Singer   Little Man with the Big Horn
Hartley Toots' Harlem Swing Band
They Put You in the Grove — and Keep You There!
One Night Only – Sun., Mar. 31, 12:01-4
TOP HAT   ADM. 65c

The nightly fare at the club featured a well-staged and choreographed floorshow. One of the most memorable acts was the return of Atlanta's favorite: the Whitman Sisters and their show "Harlem to Atlanta," which featured a cast of 60 performers direct from Harlem and seen here in an advertisement. Admission to the show ranged between 40¢ and 65¢, and there were two shows nightly. (Courtesy of *Atlanta Daily World,* c. 1940.)

17

The Red McAllister Band played regularly at the Top Hat Club. Red McAllister appears at the far right. (Courtesy of Digging It Up Archives.)

On this night, couples move gracefully on the dance floor of the Top Hat Club, *c.* 1930s.

Other bands and musicians who played in the club included Snookum Russell, the Hep Cats, Tiny Bradshaw (shown here with promoter B.B. Beamon), the Bama State Revelers, Hassie Domineck's Ambassadors, Austell "Buttercup" Allen, Fletcher Henderson, the International Sweethearts of Rhythm, Neal Montgomery, Levi Mann and the Ambassadors, Don Albert, Speed Webb, and the Hollywood Blue Devils. (Courtesy of B.B. Beamon.)

Alluring Star of "Hallelujah"
Nina Mae Mc Kinney
And Her
MODERNISTIC JAZZ ORCHESTRA
Tomorrow, January 12, 9-1
ADMISSION 55c
Sunday, January 14, 12:01-4
TOP HAT   **Adm. 65c**

Movie actress and singer Nina Mae McKinney was one of hundreds of nationally known entertainers who performed at the Top Hat Club. Others were Cab Calloway, the Irving Miller Brownskin Models, Fletcher Henderson, the Carolina Cotton Pickers, and Dwight "Gatemouth" Moore. (Courtesy of Digging It Up Archives.)

Practically every social club, fraternity, and sorority competed to book and reserve space for their annual dances. Groups such as the Eight Racketeers, Alpha Phi Alpha (pictured), Kappa Alpha Psi, Phi Beta Sigma, and Omega Psi Phi Fraternities held their dances there. "When the Top Hat opened, it became the place where everybody migrated to have a dance—if you were a member, let's say of the Masons or some fraternity and your group wanted to give a dance," recalled Edwin Driskell. Even the Atlanta Coca-Cola Bottling Company held their banquet there in 1945 for its "colored" employees. (Courtesy of Griff Davis and Digging It Up Archives.)

The parents of these Spelman graduates in the Class of 1944 gave their daughters a party at the Top Hat Club. (Courtesy of Griff Davis and Digging It Up Archives.)

This unidentified social group posed on the Top Hat's dance floor. (Courtesy of B.B. Beamon.)

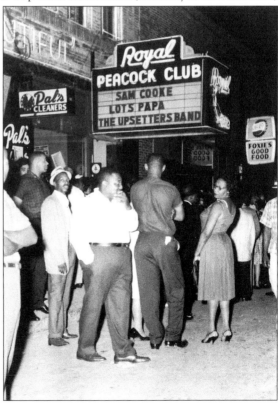

In the fall of 1949, the Top Hat closed, only to reopen a few months later as the Royal Peacock. After a successful 12-year run with the Top Hat Club, owners Blayton, Yates, and Milton decided to sell the club. Carrie Cunningham was interested in acquiring the club for her son Red McAllister so that he could stay off the dangerous, segregated roads with his band (there was often trouble and arrests on the roads for McAllister and his boys). Mrs. Cunningham paid $31,000 for the second floor of the building on Auburn Avenue, and redecorated so that it would accommodate 350 patrons. (Courtesy of Digging It Up Archives.)

On October 21, 1949, "Miss Carrie" (above) reopened the club as the Royal Peacock, with her son as manager. Red McAllister, who operated a talent agency located in the Hooper Building, had booked Paul Gayten and his orchestra for the opening show through his contact with the Gale Agency. Gayten's orchestra featured former Atlantan Annie Laura (right), who began her career while a student at Booker T. Washington High School. She worked with Eddie Heywood and Andy Fairchild as the star of Sammy Green's company, which performed at theaters in Atlanta and Birmingham. Ms. Laura also sang with Snookum Russell and was the star of a revue at the Plantation Club in Los Angeles, performing for two and a half years. (Courtesy of Digging It Up Archives.)

Carrie Cunningham's life as a businesswoman was as rich as the colors of the peacocks that she was infatuated with. Born in Atlanta, she began the foray in the entertainment world as a circus rider in the Silas Greene Traveling Show. After the traveling show days, she acquired some property on Decatur Street and rented rooms. Later she acquired the upstairs portion over the Citizens Trust Bank and opened the Royal Hotel (pictured here), where many of the performers stayed. Over the years, the lobby would become plastered with black-and-white, 8-by-10 glossies of entertainers who stayed and played at the Peacock. Not only did she operate the hotel, but she helped to manage the club in the evening; also, she was said to have been very generous, often helping to make costumes, lending musicians money, and stocking up on their favorite foods. Whenever vaudeville comedians Butterbeans and Suzy would come to Atlanta, Ms. Cunningham would have already filled a tin tub with ice and beer and have it waiting for them.

Another legend born in the annals of the Royal Peacock who benefited from Ms. Cunningham and Red McAllister was gutsy rhythm and blues singer Big Maybelle. Born Mary Belle (Mabel) Smith in Jackson, Tennessee, she began her career in 1945 with Red McAllister's band, where she sang for him for several years before going to Indiana to go solo. A Royal Peacock regular, she and Willie Mae Thornton were two of the legendary "blues shouters." According to legend, Thornton introduced the song "Hound Dog," later made popular by Elvis Presley. During one of Big Maybelle's appearances in Atlanta, she forgot to bring her outfits, and, according to lore, Carrie Cunningham pulled some draperies from a window and stitched her an outfit. (Courtesy of Digging It Up Archives.)

There is perhaps not a major entertainer who performed in Atlanta during the 1940s to the 1970s who did not perform at the Royal Peacock. The diversity and variety of talent that walked across the Peacock's stage perhaps cannot be matched by any other club, other than the ones in the North. The early days of the Peacock were a spillover from the Top Hat Club. It featured full-scale floorshows, emcees, comedians, chorus girls, shake girls, and always one major act. Many clubs and organizations held their annual dances there, as did the Pals Social Club (pictured here) in 1952. (Courtesy of Digging It Up Archives.)

The Royal Peacock was later acquired by Henry Wynn (center), who booked some of the top acts in the business through his Supersonic Attractions agency for the Peacock and brought in local musicians to perform backup for many of the entertainers. Q.P. Jones Jr. managed the Peacock from 1959 to 1965. Wynn reopened the newly renovated club in November 1960 as the New Royal Peacock and had secured Bill Doggett as his star act. But on the day of the grand reopening, Doggett was unable to make it and organist Wild Bill Davis performed. Comedian Flip Wilson performed at the Royal Peacock while being mustered at Fort McPherson. (Courtesy of Digging It Up Archives.)

Lloyd Terry, whose band performed on the stage of the Royal Peacock, remembered that Monday nights at the club was "Hustler's Night." Most of the waiters and waitresses that worked in downtown establishments during the week flocked to the Peacock on that particular weekend night. Shown above are members of the staff of the New Royal Peacock. (Courtesy of the *Atlanta Inquirer*.)

Today, Patti Labelle electrifies Atlanta audiences at the Fox Theater and Chastain Park. But during the 1960s, Patti Labelle (right) and the Bluebells brought their harmonious melodies and their "hair" to the Royal Peacock's stage.

Left: Sam Cooke was a regular visitor to Atlanta. Here he is shown between sets mixing with the audience at the Royal Peacock.

Right: James Brown and Jackie Wilson (at right) were Royal Peacock regulars. Here they are shown in a rare photograph together, *c.* 1950s. Brown who would become "the Godfather of Soul" was born in Augusta, Georgia, and perfected his craft as an entertainer in small juke joints throughout Georgia and the South. He was a regular at the Lithonia Country Club during the early 1950s. By the 1960s, he was performing to sold-out audiences at the City Auditorium and the Atlanta Stadium. (Courtesy of Digging It Up Archives.)

Ike and Tina Turner and their revue performed at the Royal Peacock in 1965. In addition to those already listed, a vast array of entertainers performed on the Peacock stage in the 1950s and 1960s, including Memphis Slim, Muddy Waters, Little Richard, Fats Domino, B.B. King, Dakota Staton, Frankie Lymon, Gene Chandler, Joe Simon, Jerry Butler, Arthur Prysock, Chuck Jackson, Mary Wells, and many others.

By the 1970s, Auburn Avenue began to decline and the Royal Peacock's popularity and image also declined drastically due to desegregation and urban renewal in the area surrounding the street. In the image below, even the marquee shows the years of wear and tear. The club, still operating in the 1990s, now caters to reggae and hip-hop music. (Courtesy of the Lane Brothers Collection/Georgia State University and Digging It Up Archives.)

The City of Atlanta replaced the old 1909 Auditorium Armory after fire damaged a large portion of the facility and constructed a new Municipal Auditorium in the 1930s. The hall, formerly known as Taft Hall, was the site of some of the greatest shows in the history of the city. Located upstairs was a smaller facility known as Taft Hall, which was used for smaller dances and parties. (Courtesy of Digging It Up Archives.)

For larger shows, concerts, and dances, local promoters rented out the City Auditorium. J. Neal Montgomery, a teacher at Booker T. Washington High School and a band leader, began to book and promote acts at the auditorium in the 1940s with his Southeastern Artists company. Even Tom Bailey, brother of the late Charles Bailey, also booked acts outside of their famous 81 Theater on Decatur Street.

Advertisements like this one appeared throughout the *Atlanta Daily World*. (Courtesy of the *Atlanta Daily World*.)

Local promoters brought such popular acts as Cab Calloway and Louis Armstrong (seen here) to the City Auditorium. In 1934, Louis Armstrong and Duke Ellington and his 15-piece orchestra "rocked" the City Auditorium with his vocalist Ivie Anderson (Armstrong would later return under the Southeastern Artist promotion). The show also offered a 30-minute amateur contest featuring the Mills Brothers, impersonators, and demonstrations of the dance "Snake Hips." (Courtesy of Digging It Up Archives.)

Musicians such as Fletcher Henderson, Noble Sissle, and Duke Ellington (shown with his band) were so popular with both races that when they brought their bands to the City Auditorium in July 1935, a special section of the auditorium was reserved for white patrons to hear their music. The previous year, Ellington's concert at the auditorium attracted 8,000 people. Those attending shoved, elbowed, and pushed their way inside. Over 3,000 disappointed fans were lined outside on Courtland Street. After intermission, about 700 left due to being cramped, and the box office reopened, selling tickets to people who would replace those who left. Monitored by 16 policemen, Duke Ellington was one of the most popular entertainers to perform in Atlanta. (Courtesy of Edwin Driskell.)

Louis Jordan and his band faces a packed house at the City Auditorium, c. 1940s. (Courtesy of Digging It Up Archives.)

Noble Sissle enjoyed coming to Atlanta, where he performed at the City Auditorium. He visited friends and family, including his sister who lived in the city and was married to Dr. Hutton, a prominent educator and officer of the Georgia State Teacher's Association. Sissle also visited his old army buddy Walter H. "Chief" Aiken, who was one of Atlanta's leading citizens and would later book entertainment acts for his jazz club at the Waluhaje Hotel. (Courtesy of Digging It Up Archives.)

DANCE

with

Cab Calloway

and His Cotton Club Orchestra

IN PERSON

CITY AUDITORIUM

Thurs., Sept. 13th, 9 p. m. Til ?   Adm. 65c, Tax. Inc

Many of the entertainers played more than one performance while in the city. In many cases, they performed to both white and black audiences as Cab Calloway did in September 1934, when white promoter G. Tom Bailey played Calloway at the Shrine Mosque Ballroom for an all-white Election Night dance and the following night at the City Auditorium for "colored" people only. Most of the nightclubs and venues were segregated; however, there were some such as the Top Hat Club, later the Royal Peacock, which had a special night for white patrons, usually on Saturday night. (Courtesy of the *Atlanta Daily World.*)

Noted writer Lawrence D. Reddick recalls one of Dizzy Gillespie's visits to Atlanta. Uncertain of local race relations etiquette in Atlanta, Reddick had vowed that he would not patronize any Jim Crow theaters or gatherings. However, a new music form, "be-bop," interested him, and the "Bop King" was in town. At this concert at the City Auditorium, blacks and whites were sitting on the auditorium main floor. The auditorium was only half-filled. Reddick attributed it to the inclement weather but observed that when the "Silas Green from New Orleans" show appeared the week before, it was packed and the weather was not that much better. Reddick saw that the blacks present were younger than the whites. (Courtesy of Digging It Up Archives.)

However, even this calm atmosphere could not convince Nat King Cole (shown with B.B. Beamon [second from left] and wife, Maria) to fulfill a concert engagement in Atlanta at the City Auditorium in April 1952, following a racial incident in Birmingham, Alabama. Appearing at Birmingham's Municipal Auditorium, Cole was assaulted when six men rushed onto the stage. This incident placed fear in Cole, who said that he was afraid to come to Atlanta because it was so close to Birmingham; Cole stated that he would not come to Atlanta for a "million dollars." Cole had been watching television and saw pictures of the Klu Klux Klan in Macon, Georgia, and the newspapers were full of segregation articles.

The all-female band International Sweethearts of Rhythm were an Atlanta favorite and regular performers at the City Auditorium.

Left: "Mr. B," the fabulous Billy Eckstine, shown here on the stage of the City Auditorium, was a regular performer in Atlanta during the 1940s. (Courtesy of Digging It Up Archives.)
Right: Louis Jordan brought his Tymphanny Five to the City Auditorium many times and performed favorites such as "Reet Petite." (Courtesy of Digging It Up Archives.)

The Clovers entertain the audience at the City Auditorium. Other entertainers included Earl "Fatha" Hines, the Mills Brothers, the Ink Spots, Dorothy Maynor, Ethel Waters, Eddie Rochester, Lena Horne, Marian Anderson, "Hot Lips" Page, Stepin Fetchit, Billie Holiday, King Cole Trio, and Lionel Hampton. (Courtesy of Clarence Hubbard.)

Ruth Brown and Atlanta comedian Al Jackson "clown it up" backstage at the City Auditorium, c. 1954. (Courtesy of Harmon Perry.)

In July 1951, Josephine Baker canceled her planned performance because she could not obtain first-class accommodations at one of the city's major hotels. Miss Baker had accepted the invitation extended by Walter White and the NAACP on June 30 with the condition that she and her party be housed in a first-class hotel, that there be no segregation in the audience, and that a mixed orchestra provide music. On Monday, May 5, 1951, Walter White unsuccessfully wired three of Atlanta's leading hotels asking for reservations for three days for Miss Baker and her party. Walter White urged Miss Baker to go on with the performance since two of her conditions had been met. Miss Baker wired a response stating the following: "It makes my heart beat with happiness to know that you not only appreciate but agree to my keeping my principles in not going to Atlanta because the hotels have refused my accommodations to me and my party. The fact of being in a white hotel does not flatter me in the least, but it is a matter of being a Negro and not being able to go wherever you desire. This situation grieves me deeply and I am all heart with you and the NAACP, Dr. Bunch and all of our people who are fighting to conquer injustice, discrimination and prejudice against people who only want to be considered as human beings. I profoundly believe in God and am absolutely certain we will win."

You could get to the Sunset by streetcar. Hundreds came nightly and on weekends to hear local bands such as Wayman Carver's Orchestra, Neal Montgomery, the Troubadours, the Southern Ramblers, and many others who entertained on its stage during the 1930s and 1940s. In 1937, Ella Fitzgerald and Chick Webb lit up the Sunset Casino. The era of the Big Band sound ushered in many local and national bands on the stage of the casino. Weekly Jitterbug contests were held, and dances from New York such as the "Big Apple," "the Lindy Hop," "the Suzi Q," and "the Peeking" were introduced to Atlantans at the Sunset. Admission ranged from 25¢ to $1 depending on the event. The management of the casino changed hands frequently until local promoter and orchestra leader Neal Montgomery assumed the ownership of the dance hall. In 1944, he wrote a letter to Mayor William Hartsfield requesting that Magnolia Street be widened and paved from Davis (now Northside Drive to Chestnut Street) Street and that Sunset from Simpson to Hunter Streets be improved also.

A bevy of entertainers performed on the stage of the Sunset, including Count Basie, Jimmie Lunceford, Orlando Roberson, Bama State Collegians, Lucky Millinder, Fats Waller, Don Redman, Sister Rosetta Tharpe, Hot Lips Hackett, Eddie Durham and his All-Star Girl Band, Little Joe and his Flashy Clouds of Rhythm, Savannah Churchill, Tiny Bradshaw, Speed Webb, and the Hollywood Blue Devils.

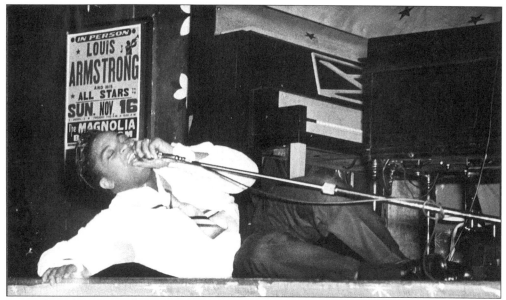

Located on the corner of Sunset Avenue and Magnolia Street was the Sunset Amusement park, which featured a large dance hall pavilion known as the Sunset Casino. The amusement park opened during the 1920s and featured an array of rides for children, a theater, and boxing arena. Col. S.R. Speede managed it. By the 1930s, the Sunset Casino was one of the most popular halls in Atlanta for large dances, concerts, and recreational sports games. It even hosted the Bell and Powell Circus in the 1930s, staged by two Atlantans and featuring high wire, skating, tight rope, trapeze, and gymnastic acts. Primary access to the Sunset was by streetcar. Above, an Atlanta favorite, Jackie Wilson, sprawled out on the stage of the Magnolia Ballroom, *c.* 1959. (Courtesy of Harmon Perry.)

The fabulous Joe Tex rocks the house during one of the thousands of shows held at the club located in Vine City. (Courtesy of Harmon Perry.)

The dance hall underwent a name change in 1947 and became one of Atlanta's largest recreational centers. Managed by Ralph Mays, who was also a band leader and musician, and later by B.B. Beamon, the Magnolia hosted every major entertainer of the late 1950s, including the Upsetters (seen here), Little Willie John, Jimmy Smith, B.B. King, T-Bone Walker, Roy Milton, Erskine Hawkins, Bill Doggett, Ray Charles, Etta James, Gloria Lynne, Ray Charles Lloyd Price, the Flames, Muddy Waters, Jerry Butler, Louis Jordan, Bobby Bland, Bo Didley, Little Richard, comedian Dick Gregory, and Chuck Berry, who in his autobiography recalled witnessing a shooting at the club in May 1958. Berry had decided to visit the club after performing at the Whiskey Club in Atlanta. (Courtesy of Count Jackson.)

The legendary "Lady Day," or Billie Holiday (seen here at left), performed at the Magnolia in March 1959, three months before her death. Miss Holiday is pictured with B.B. Beamon and an unidentified guest. Jazz was a popular medium at the Magnolia. Jazz artists such as Art Blakely and the Jazz Messenger, Stan Keaton, and Lionel Hampton performed there. (Courtesy of B.B. Beamon.)

The Shriners Annual Dance was held at the Magnolia; members of one of the local chapters appear here c. 1959.

The Bronzemen Club members posed for this picture during their annual dance at the Magnolia Ballroom, c. 1950s.

The Magnolia was rented by fraternities and sororities for their anniversary dances. The facility was also used for basketball games and intramural tournaments. Practically every social club in Atlanta held an anniversary dance, like the Grand Beauticians' Ball or the NAACP's Freedom Ball, at the Magnolia Ballroom every Friday or Saturday night when a national act was not appearing. The Shriners Bathing Beauty Contest and the Bronner Brother Fashion and HairStyle Revue were both held there. The Lloyd Terry Band provides the musical entertainment for the Bronzemen annual dance (at left). (Courtesy of Charles and Clara Lowe/Digging It Up Archives.)

The Lloyd Terry Band (above) played for many different social groups on the stage of the Magnolia; they are, from left to right, as follows: McClellan Smith, Jimmy Newman, Gladys Knight, and Billy Reid, c. 1958. Lloyd Terry (not shown) recalled when Gladys was 14 years old that her repertoire included songs such as "Doodling" and numerous tunes written by Paul Mitchell, William Braynon, and Duke Pearson, which she performed with the band. A show announcement (right) from the Magnolia features Little Richard for a performance on December 25, 1955.

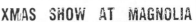

XMAS SHOW AT MAGNOLIA

LITTLE WALTER   LITTLE RICHARD

LITTLE WALTER
AND HIS   JUKES

LITTLE RICHARD
'THE TOOTIE FRUITIE MAN'

The SPIDERS

TODAY & MON: DEC. 25 & 26
TWO SHOWS TODAY, DECEMBER 25
First Show 5 P. M. -:- Second Show 9 P. M.

DANCING, MONDAY DECEMBER 26th
8:30 P. M. TO 12:30 A. M.

MAGNOLIA BALLROOM
Admission $1.25

During the Civil Rights Movement in the 1960s, the Magnolia was the site of mass meetings and public programs. The Honorable Elijah Muhammad, leader of the Nation of Islam, made his only Atlanta appearance at the Magnolia Ballroom on Sunday, September 11, 1960. A forum on "Black Unity: The Key to Freedom" was held with over 650 persons in attendance. The concrete block building was razed in the early 1970s and today is just a vacant lot. (Courtesy of Harmon Perry.)

Bobby "Blue" Bland crooned many tunes on the stage of the Magnolia Ballroom.

CLUB POINCIANA

And Its Staff Wishes You A Merry Christmas and Happy New Year

WILLIAM COATES
Director

O. P. JONES
Manager

RUBY DABNEY, Entertainer

Ring Out The Old Year, Ring In The New At The . . . .

CLUB POINCIANA

The Club Poinciana was opened in the 1940s by Bill Smith, with Johnny Johnson as the first manager. William Coates later joined the establishment, along with Q.P. Jones and J.B. Stroud. After Coates and Jones dissolved their business ties, Jones, along with his wife, Alyce "Sweet" Jones, managed the club. Billy Wright (seen in the advertisement reprinted from the *Atlanta Pictorial Reporter* on the next page) was a regular performer at the club. During the war years, the Club Poinciana was so popular that many nights following a show at the City Auditorium, the musicians would come and perform late-night sets at the Poinciana and crowds would fill the house. It was said to have had one of the best floorshows in the city. It was very popular with white audiences, though segregation laws prevented them from mixing with the blacks. A typical 1940s lineup featured the Billy Valentine Trio and dancers Ray Sneed Jr., Cora Bell Scruggs, Ruby Calhoun, and Louis Diggs. (Reprinted from the *Atlanta Daily World*.)

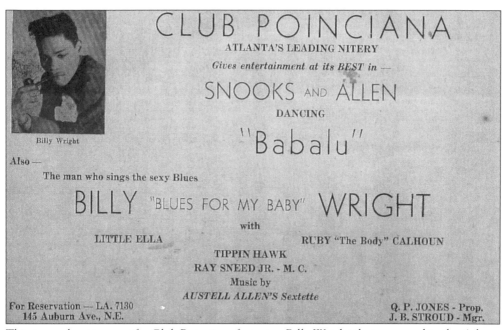

This is an advertisement for Club Poinciana featuring Billy Wright that appeared in the *Atlanta Pictorial Reporter*, *c.* 1947.

Velma "Chubby" Newsom, also known as the "Hip Shakin Mama," performed at the Club Poinciana in 1947. She had come from the Club Casino in Detroit, Michigan. Featured in her show were Billy Wright and Jimmy Lot and his Merry Makers with vocalist Tippin Hawk. (Courtesy of Digging It Up Archives.)

Three young ladies stand on Auburn Avenue near the entrance of the Club Poinciana sign, *c.* 1940s. After the decline of the club, Q.P. Jones opened and operated Pal's Cleaners and Shoeshine Parlor below the Royal Peacock Club. He later remodeled the old service station at Auburn and Bell Street and opened another Pal's Cleaners. Jones was a member of Allen Temple A.M.E. Church and a contributor to the Community Chest, Atlanta Negroes Voters League, and the YMCA. By the late 1950s, the club closed and was reopened later as the Morocco Lounge and Club by Henry Wynn. J.P. Foster managed the club in 1950 until he was charged with firing his pistol at the floor during a dispute with patrons who objected to being searched before going in for the show. The building was owned by the *Atlanta Daily World*, which moved its operations to the site. (Courtesy of William Calloway.)

Several night spots were located on Simpson Road, including the popular Lincoln Country Club, Music in the Trees, and Butler Paradise (later renamed the Congo Club). The Lincoln clubhouse, which opened in the 1920s, was adjacent to the golf course then located on the outskirts of the city limit. (Courtesy of Digging It Up Archives.)

A few blocks down from the golf course was Music in the Trees and Butler's Paradise, 1.5 miles from Ashby Street. A drive-in restaurant, Butler's Paradise featured a floorshow. A 1945 advertisement indicated that music was provided by Waymon C. Brown and his orchestra. Music in the Trees was another club on Simpson Road. With speakers in the trees, it was one of the first open-air entertainment spots. It was across from the Chita Chata Restaurant. By the 1960s, the American Legion, the Boom Boom Room, and the Crescendo Club had opened and featured among its many entertainers Rudy Wellmaker and his combo and the Esby Whitehead Combo. (Reprinted from the *Atlanta Daily World.*)

This is an advertisement for the opening of the Turf Lounge on Simpson Road, *c*. 1960s. The club was owned by Howard Jefferson and James Hughley. (Reprinted from the *Atlanta Inquirer*.)

Turf Lounge and Restaurant

2079 Simpson Road, N.W.
794-9213
NOW OPEN MONDAY THRU SATURDAY 9A.M. to 2A.M.

Atlanta's Newest And Finest

Opening Nite At Turf

SPACIOUS, SWANK, DINING ROOM

THE PROPRIETORS —
Mr. Howard Jefferson receives a beautiful boutonniere from his wife and Mr. James Hughey also receives a beautiful boutonniere from his wife.

LOUNGE and BAR

Entertainment Nightly
Cocktail Hours
Daily 2 – 8:30 P.M.

Tuesday Night Is Filly Night
Wednesday Night Is Stud Night
Serving Your Favorite Beverage

MAKE YOUR RESERVATION FOR CHRISTMAS AND NEW YEAR'S EVE PARTY

The USO Club, located near Washington High School on C Street, was a popular entertainment facility during the war years. After the club closed down, Washington High used it as a snack bar. The building was later demolished and an auditorium for the school was built on its spot. (Reprinted from the *Atlanta Daily World*/Digging It Up Archives.)

This a picture of the Alpha Phi Alpha fraternity's annual New Year's Eve Dance at the USO Club, *c.* 1940s.

The Lithonia Country Club, which opened in the 1940s, was located in DeKalb County, on the property of the Lithonia Speedway. Entertainers such as Little Richard, Bobby "Blue" Bland, Elmore James and Little Walter, B.B. King, James Brown, and Lotsa Poppa cut their teeth at the country club during the 1950s. Grady "Fats" Jackson (shown here) had the house band at the Lithonia Country Club. He also served as the president of the Atlanta Musicians Protective Association Local 463. (Courtesy of Harmon Perry.)

This is an advertisement for the Elks Club's "Boogie Revue," featuring Ruby Calhoun, Perlene Ellison, and others, c. 1937. (Reprinted from the *Atlanta Daily World*.)

During the decade of the 1940s, Auburn Avenue was the home of several popular clubs including the Elks Club and the Congo Club, which opened in 1947 and was located on the corner of Houston and Piedmont. The Congo Club was managed by Ellis Ferrell and featured a variety of local and national performers, including Velma "Chubby" Newsome, Billy Wright, and Jimmy Lot and his Merrymakers. Each Monday, the "Blue Monday" party was held. The Elks Social Club was located at 73 Fort Street. (Courtesy of Digging It Up Archives)

Irvin Favor opened the Club Zanzibar at Auburn Avenue as a family affair. A full-course dinner was served from 8:00 a.m. to 4:00 p.m. During its early years the club was managed by Robert Morris. A line-up for one of the 1947 shows included dancers Nikki and Rikki, Bobby Steven, Clay Bray, and music by the Zanzibarons. Katherine Jefferson, who worked for the House of Murphy printers, printer of many of the show posters, recalled going to the Zanzibar one evening when Billy Wright was headlining. She recalled seeing a young man sweeping the floor only to stop during intermission to perform. She did not realize his name until she began printing placards for him. His name was Little Richard. Pictured below are, from left to right, as follows: Irvin Favors, Miranda Favors (his wife), Irvin Favors Jr. (his son), and Robert Morris (the club manager), c. 1949. (Courtesy of Digging It Up Archives.)

Irvin Favor owned several businesses on Auburn Avenue, including Champs' Pool Room and the Auburn Avenue One-Hour Cleaner before opening the Auburn Avenue Casino in July 1956, which was located directly across the street from the Royal Peacock. He added a large ballroom to the already existing building and created what he would call the Rainbow Room. The seating capacity was 700, which made it the largest ballroom in the downtown area. The casino featured a Las Vegas–themed lobby with slot machines and other gambling decor. The club also had a private room called the Rainbow Terrace for smaller private affairs. During its opening week, the casino featured a gospel fest to draw listeners of gospel music, as well as popular rhythm and blues acts, comediennes, and dances. The opening act for the club was Laverne Baker and the Roy Mays Orchestra. Miss Baker, who popularized the song "Tweedle Dee" and "I Cried a Tear," worked as a dancer with the Royal Peacock Chorus line and was billed as "Little Miss Sharecropper" before branching out and developing her singing career. Because of the size of the facility, it was a popular meeting space. Bronner Brothers Hair Care Products held their Hair Conventions and Shows in the its auditorium. The Auburn Avenue Casino closed in the 1970s. The casino reopened in 1996 during the Centennial Olympic Games and is now a popular spot for hip hop shows and dances. (Courtesy of Skip Mason.)

Laverne Baker (top left) opened the Auburn Avenue Casino. Shown at the bottom left is the front entrance of the Auburn Avenue Casino, c. 1960s. Note the marquee features Major Lance in concert. Major Lance (top right) returned to Atlanta, where he lived until his death in 1995. (Courtesy of Harmon Perry.)

Dancers crowd the dance floor of the Auburn Avenue Casino doing the popular dance "the Continental," c. 1960. (Courtesy of Digging It Up Archives.)

Delegates at the annual Bronner Brother's Convention inside of the Casino Ballroom were photographed c. 1959. The casino had one of the largest spaces for different African-American events in Atlanta. (Courtesy of Digging It Up Archives.)

Mr. Favors began an annual tradition of using the club to present gifts to needy children in the community. (Courtesy of the Favors family.)

Motown star Marvin Gaye performed his hit tunes in Atlanta during the 1960s at the Royal Peacock. At one memorable performance, he appeared in a blue suede suit.

The Atlanta University Center Schools held many dances for the students and featured live bands. Seen here is the Morehouse College Homecoming Dance, which took place in the school's gymnasium, c. 1955.

Seen here in this 1960s photograph are some musicians standing at the Cave, which was located on Piedmont Avenue. (Courtesy of Clarence Hubbard.)

This photograph shows a group enjoying a night at the Cave.

The American Legion had several popular night spots throughout Atlanta, including Post 508, which was located on Piedmont Avenue. Performing above is Allen Murphy (behind the microphone), c. 1950s. Murphy was a local boy raised on Tatnall Street in Atlanta's Westside.

As African Americans began to move out to the suburbs of Adamsville and Collier Heights, B.B. Beamon and Herman Nash decided to build a club that would cater to this new rising middle class. Located in northwest Atlanta at 3160 Bankhead Highway, the Paladium Club opened in July 1965 and featured as its opening acts Brook Benton, Cannonball Adderley and his orchestra, and Laverne Baker. A few of the entertainers who would grace the stage included Gloria Lynn, Aretha Franklin, Joe Tex, Ahmad Jamal, King Curtis, Margie Hendrix, Nina Simone, Jimmy McGriff, Roland Kirk, Barbara Lewis, Arthur Prysock, Johnny Nash, Gloria Gaynor, Dee Warwick, Les McCann, Roy Hamilton, Jimmy Reed, the Coasters, Betty Everett, Major Lance, Lionel Hampton, Johnny Nash, and Ray Charles, shown here with his revue, c. 1966.

Appearing Last Times Tonight

AT
ATLANTA'S NEWEST AND FINEST NIGHT SPOT

The Fabulous New

CLUB PALADIUM

★

Aretha Franklin
And Her Trio

The future "Queen of Soul" Aretha Franklin began coming to Atlanta as a teenager with her father, Reverend C.L. Franklin, singing at the gospel concerts at the old City Auditorium. By the 1960s, as she moved into jazz and rhythm and blues, Aretha performed at the Royal Peacock, the Paladium (above), and Paschal's La Carrousel.

During a Hungry Club Forum in February 1958 at the Butler Street YMCA, Dr. Willis Lawrence James, head of the music department at Spelman and Morehouse Colleges, defined the music form of jazz. Speaking on the topic "Jazz: Yesterday and Today," James cited that "Negro folk songs and jazz music had come from a culture which originated in the United States and not in Europe and that it was accepted as 'total American.'" James spoke of the roots of jazz as a blending of two cultures, European and African, and that it was produced out of the feeling of people. James's wisdom may have been a foresight to the influx of jazz clubs that would be opened during the fifties and sixties in the African-American communities in Atlanta.

Jazz legend Duke Ellington (seen above, second from left), an Atlanta regular, is greeted at the front desk of the Waluhaje Hotel (c. 1950s) by its owners, "Chief" Walter Aiken (far left); his wife, Lucy (third from left); and her sister Jenny (far right). The jazz club at the Waluhaje was one of the hottest in town. The building was named for its owners, using the first letters of their names: WAlter, LUcy, HAzle, and JEnny. (Courtesy of the Atlanta History Center.)

The Waluhaje Ballroom catered strictly to jazz music and featured the outstanding jazz musicians of the world, including Lionel Hampton, Duke Ellington, Dizzy Gillespie, Woody Herman, Earl Bostic, Stan Getz, and Dinah Washington, as well as the best in local talent. The club became known as the Jazz Mecca and was a popular place for social functions for local clubs and organizations. Mr. and Mrs. Leroy Johnson and Mr. and Mrs. Calvin "Monk" Jones are shown in the Bamboo Room at the Waluhaje. (Courtesy of Clarence Hubbard.)

An Atlanta favorite, Billie Holiday receives flowers from a grateful patron during a performance at the Waluhaje. She made her last performance at the Waluhaje in April 1951, three months before her death in July at the age of 44. White Atlantans were also attracted to the Waluhaje to catch its big acts, such as Billie Holiday, and would often intermingle with the black patrons, even though it was illegal for blacks and whites to socialize in public. According to Jack Gibson, "during one of Dizzy Gillespie sets, Police Chief Herbert Jenkins came in and using a rope divided the club and asked the whites to sit on one side and the blacks on the other side. If they did not adhere to that, he threatened to close the club even though he patronized it frequently."

Musicians Edward Emory (saxophone), Norris Jones (bass), George Jordan (piano), and Buzzy Jones (drums) perform at Buddy Gloss's Place on Chestnut Street. (Courtesy of Edward Emory.)

Here, Edward Emory (saxophone) and others jam at the Builders Club.

The Continental Lounge was located at 813 Hunter Street, near the Cooper Service Station. Some of the entertainers who performed there included Otis Collier, Donald Bell, the exotic dancer Vivian, Ernie Ford, and Danny Woods. The club was managed by P. Roguemore. Shown here is a band performing at the lounge, *c.* 1960. Milton Howard (center) is on guitar. By 1963, this spot was also known as the Kitty Kat Lounge.

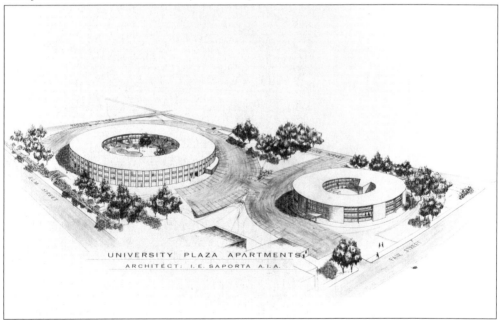

After the construction of the University Apartments on Fair Street, a jazz club opened called the "Bird Cage." It was a very popular, cozy, and intimate club and bar, providing another venue for jazz music. National entertainers such as Cannonball Adderly performed there. Today the facility is a part of the Clark Atlanta University Residential Living. (Courtesy of Digging It Up Archives.)

The Donn Clendenon's Supper Club opened in the 1960s. Owned by Atlantan and major league baseball player Donn Clendenon, the club was a popular spot on Hunter Street. (Courtesy of Digging It Up Archives.)

Paschal La Carrousel was opened on December 3, 1960, by Robert and James Paschal (seen here), proprietors of Paschal's Restaurant, as a small and intimate jazz club, adjacent to their restaurant on Hunter Street. (Courtesy of James Paschal.)

La Carrousel's seating capacity was 600, and during the 1960s, it rapidly gained popularity as a meeting place for friends and out-of-town guests and a spot for some of the best jazz in the city. Monday nights featured the Blue Monday Jam Session. (Courtesy of James Paschal.)

The entertainment at La Carrousel featured a mixture of locally known talent and nationally recognized musicians, including Stanley Turrentine, Jimmy Smith, Aretha Franklin, the Ramsey Lewis Trio, Dizzy Gillespie, Lou Rawls, Bill Doggett, Yusef Lateef, Wynton Kelly, and the Paul Mitchell Trio. (Courtesy of James Paschal.)

Mitchell's musical career began at Morris Brown College, and he later played in the army band. A former high school band director, Mitchell was known for his arrangement of music. He later became a fixture at Dante's Down the Hatch at the old Underground and in Buckhead.

Mrs. Orah Bell Sherman (shown here) began her career as a hostess at the Builders Club before going to La Carrousel. Christine Hunter and her husband, Clifford, known as "Fats," were entrepreneurs who also owned a recording studio and operated the popular Builders Club at 507 Kennedy Street in the Vine City community near Northside Drive. Practically every Atlanta musician played the club. On Sundays, it featured a hot jam session.

The Sahara Club, located on Chestnut Street, specialized in great jazz music. (Courtesy of Clarence Hubbard.)

Though not a large lounge, the Town Club was located at 55 Northside Drive in the University Motel complex during the 1950s and 1960s. It was rumored that the Town Club was owned by entertainer Ray Charles, who financed the club for a friend. (Courtesy of the Lane Brothers Collection/Georgia State University.)

There were several large outdoor venues used to house large concerts, including the old Ponce De Leon Ballpark on Ponce De Leon Avenue, Washington Park, Herndon Stadium on Vine Street, and the Atlanta Stadium. The stadium was constructed as an athletic facility for Morris Brown College in 1947. It was named the Alonzo Franklin Memorial Stadium and was a gift to Morris Brown College from Norris B. Herndon and the Herndon Foundation. President William Fountain Jr. conceived the idea of establishing a stadium after he became disenchanted with the fact that the football team had to travel to Ponce De Leon Park for its home football games. Norris Herndon donated an estimated $500,000 for the construction of the stadium.

But the stadium was more than just an athletic facility for sporting events. Some of the best-known entertainers graced its grounds. It served as a larger venue for concerts and rallies and the likes of gospel singer Mahalia Jackson, Clara Ward, Ray Charles, and James Brown. B.B. Beamon's annual Big Show of Stars brought entertainers such as Sam Cooke, the Everly Brothers, Clyde McPhatter, Georgie Hamilton IV, Lavern Baker, Frankie Avalon, the Silhouettes, the Royal Teens, Jackie Wilson, the Monotones, the Crescendos, the Storey Sisters, Jimmy Reed, Chubby Checker, the Drifters, Bo Didley, Ben. E. King, Chuck Jackson, the Shells, Paul Williams and his show of stars orchestra, and Harold Cromer, who was the master of ceremonies. In 1959, Ray Charles recorded a live album at Herndon Stadium.

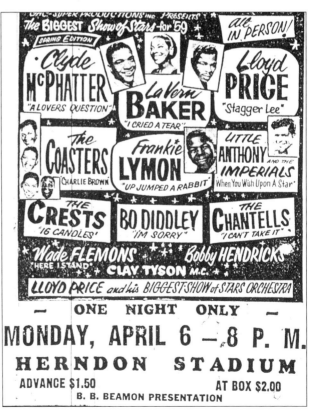

Over at the old Ponce De Leon Park, large shows were produced. The radio station WAKE presented its first Southeastern Jazz Festival in 1962, which featured Dave Brubeck; the Oscar Peterson Trio; Lionel Hampton; John Lee Hooker; the Dick Clark Show, featuring the Crystals, Johnny Tillotson, Dick and Dee, and Ruby and the Romantics; Ray Charles and the Raylettes; Jackie Wilson; Fats Domino; Ben. E. King; the Orlons; the Drifters; Gladys Knight and the Pips; the Temptations; and Stevie Wonder—all these artists performed under the oaks at the old ballpark.

Two
The Patrons

"Folks balled every weekend," according to Jondelle Johnson, a social columnist for the *Atlanta Inquirer* during the 1960s who covered the social events of the clubs and organizations in her column "Around Atlanta." Each week since the 1920s, Atlantans have been informed of the social happenings through its local newspapers. The *Atlanta Daily World* featured the Society Slants and Social Swirl columns with columnists Alice Marie, Lucious Jones, Marjorie Fowlkes, Alice Washington, and the dean of society columnists, Ozeil Fryer Woolcock. That column is now written by Herbert Bridgewater. During the 1940s, the *Atlanta Pictorial Reporter* featured a column, "Talk of the Town," written by Annie Doris Hall. Another society columnist for the *Atlanta Inquirer* was Paulyne Morgan White, who wrote the "Sparkling Specialties" column.

These journalists wrote of the dances, the soirees, the anniversary celebrations, who attended, where the events were held, the decorations, and what the band played. The photographs on the next pages are of clubgoers, patrons, and persons who enjoyed a night out at one of many clubs or dances held in Atlanta. Some of the dances were held at the major venues and others at homes such as the Tiger Flower Villa on Simpson Road, and by the 1960s, smaller clubhouses such as the Delmar Lane Clubhouse.

Mrs. Lucille McAllister Scott was a prominent socialite in Atlanta and a dear friend of Duke Ellington. She would often entertain him during his visits to Atlanta. She is shown with several entertainers and radio personality Dave Bondu (right), *c.* 1940s. (Courtesy of Lucille Scott.)

An unidentified group enjoys a night out on the town, *c.* 1950s.

This is a partial listing of some of the hundreds of social groups, bridge clubs, and organizations in the African-American community in Atlanta from the turn of the century to the 1960s compiled from the social columns of the *Atlanta Independent*, the *Atlanta Daily World*, the *Atlanta Pictorial Reporter*, the *Atlanta Voice*, and the *Atlanta Inquirer*. These groups made up many of the memorable experiences at the nightclubs for their anniversaries and dances; some of them are as follows: ABC's, Adelphi, Anges Social Club, Blue Sapphires, Bo-Peeps, Les Bon-Quieres, Bonne Temps, Bronzemen, Bulomatocs, Byous, Cameos, Cardettes, Casual Cliques, CAYA Bridge Club, Christucks, Club Acourant, Coffee Sips, Collegians Social Club, Cordozetts, Criteria Club, Crystals, Dahlia, Dames Ravsantes, Deuz Social Blu, Dixettes, Discriminating Gents, Duchess of Earls, Ebonette of Society, Ebonites, Ecoliers Social Club, Elegant Ladies, Esquires, Etucs, Exquisite Gents, Fabulous Aucourant, Femme De Chic, Flamingo Social Club Foxes, Forget Me Nots, Frauleens, Gay Y's, Gigi's, GIRLS, Glamorene Social Club, GLOB (Grand Ladies of Bridge), Gorenettes, Gone with the Wind, Heralettes, Highland Avenue Social Club, High Priests and Priestesses, Jewels, Jadettes, Jo Case, Jolly Pals, Jolly 12, Kamelyars, Klassy Kliques, Knight Kaps, Labelles, Lively Ones, Magnificent Crystals, Marvelettes, Modern Priscilla, Modernistic Social, Montes Social Club and Saving Club, MRS Club, Nomads, Orchidelles, Ortrelles, Les Petite Cherie, Pegs, Polomas, Powder Puffs, Radiant Twelve, Rollers and Rollets, Rosaree, Royal Oaks Manor, Saquinaws, Saturn Social Club, Souers, Smart Set, Sophisticated Social Club, Sophisticated Hearts, Starlettes, Suave Bronzemen, Suave Esquires, Swift Kings, Tabuettes, Twelve Sophisticated Debs, Valiant Shenenagan Social Club, Vashanettes, the Y's Men, WhatKnots Social Club, Wee Club, the Shriners, the Alphas, AKAs, Deltas, Omegas, Sigmas, Kappas, Zetas, and the Sigma Gamma Rhoers.

These four friends enjoy a night at a dance at Taft Hall in the City Auditorium, c. 1949. Identified are Noaye Smith (second from left) and Clarence Hubbard (third from left). (Reprinted from the Atlanta Voice.)

Getting ready for a night on the town are, from left to right, Deloris and Herman Mason, Betty Clifton, and Moses and Charlene Charles, c. 1957. (Courtesy of Charlene Ward.)

Three

The Promoters

Entertainers just did not show up on the doorsteps of the clubs. Bookings, arrangements, publicity, contracts, musical accompaniment, and hotel accommodations were all the responsibility of a unique group of men and women known as promoters, and throughout the decades Atlanta had a cadre of well-known personalities in the field. Some of the early promoters were L.D. Joel, S.R. Speede, W.J. Shaw, Drew Days, T. Shelton Coles, Red McAllister, Porky Slaughter, Alfred Angel, Q.P. Jones, Herman Nash, Ralph Mays, Walter Bolden, Jack Moore, and Sam Bray (the former manager of Frankie Lymon, who moved to Atlanta in 1971 and worked at the Gold Lounge on Simpson Road). However, three men—J. Neal Montgomery, B.B. Beamon, and Henry Wynn—were the most successful of the promoters in Atlanta.

J. Neal Montgomery (center) was born in the Summerhill community of Atlanta. He began a teaching career at Booker T. Washington High School in 1965. During this time he also began his music career playing in the pit band at the 81 Theater on Decatur Street and providing music for parties and dances throughout the city. The Neal Montgomery band was one of the most popular in the city. It featured some of the hottest and most talented musicians in Atlanta. Through his advocating for entertainment, Montgomery organized the Southeastern Artist Bureau, a full-scale company which presented to Atlanta virtually every nationally known band and act in the country.

Advertising played a major part in the success of the Southeastern Artist Bureau. To prepare for the arrival of Silas Green from the New Orleans show, Roderick B. Harris, executive officer of the show, wrote a detailed letter to Montgomery (left) regarding advertising and targeting the white audience for an upcoming show in November 1944. Harris reminded Montgomery to include publicity in the Sunday edition of the white newspaper theatrical page, even identifying what photographs to use and including the fact that the show had toured since 1880, that it carried its own private Pullman car, that its actors and comedians are nationally known, and that the show had played to capacity crowds for its one-night-only show.

Montgomery (left) teamed up with Jesse B. Blayton to initiate a campaign to bring prominent African Americans to Atlanta and present them in a town hall setting. Letters were mailed to Benjamin O. Davis, Adam Clayton Powell Jr., Henry Wallace, Congressman William Dawson, Howard Thurman, Wendell Wilkie, and numerous others. Honoraria would be paid. This idea was spawned by a speech given by Adam Clayton Powell Jr. at Wheat Street Baptist Church in 1946. Behind Montgomery in this picture is J. Richardson Jones, local impresario, and Graham Jackson (wearing cap), c. 1940s.

B.B. Beamon recalled the time when he spoke to J. Neal Montgomery one afternoon on Auburn Avenue during the 1940s. Montgomery did not immediately respond. Perhaps it was that Beamon had decided to enter into the entertainment promotions industry and would now become direct competition for Montgomery, who dominated the field for many years. Undaunted by the lack of friendliness, Beamon persisted and became the most successful promoter in the city. Born Burdell B. Beamon on July 27, 1916, he was the third of 14 children born to Mr. and Mrs. William Beamon in Greenwood, South Carolina. Beamon graduated from Brewer High School and joined the railroad as a dining car waiter, later arriving in Atlanta during the 1930s. During the height of his career, Beamon had established himself as a generous benefactor to local causes. Many of the proceeds from his shows benefited such groups as the Harris Memorial Hospital; the Butler Street YMCA, where he sponsored ten boys to boarding camp; and the annual School Safety Patrol Benefit Show at City Auditorium, which began in 1950. Some of Beamon's featured entertainers included Fats Domino, Ruth Brown, the Clovers, Little Willie John, and comedian Al Jackson—to name a few.

In 1954, Beamon (far left) opened the Academy of Ballet Arts on West Hunter Street. The ballet master was Hill Bermont, formerly with the Royal Academy of Dancing and the London England Ballet School. The musical director was Iona Lee Marvin. The school taught ballet, taps, and interpretive dancing. Beamon entered the promotion business around the mid-1940s, teamed with a partner named Griggs, and employed many young men, including Rusell Simmons, James Washington, and Jerry Taylor. Taylor took tickets at the door of the Sunset Casino, and Simmons worked the ticket windows and any other task that was needed. In 1950, Beamon turned over the gospel promotion to his partner Herman Nash (right), shown here with Nat King Cole, a close friend of Beamon.

In the early 1950s, Beamon leased the Magnolia Ballroom from Dr. R.A. Billings. Beamon renovated the concrete facility and began renting it out to over 500 social clubs, fraternities, and sororities. Rental fees were $16, and the groups would provide their own band and security. New life was revived in the Magnolia, as Beamon brought big-name attractions to the club. Dave Brubeck was scheduled to play the University of Georgia and had an African-American bass player. The university would not allow him to play, so the band refused to perform and played the Magnolia. Three bus loads came from Athens to the Magnolia that night. In this photograph, B.B. Beamon greets an entourage of entertainers, including Jackie "Moms" Mabley (center, wearing white hat), c. 1950s.

Some of the biggest attractions Beamon brought to Atlanta were Dinah Washington (top left), Louis Jordan (top right), and Billy Ward and the Dominoes (bottom).

B.B. King (above) and Sarah Vaughn (below) also performed at the Magnolia. Other big draws not pictured include Little Willie John, Little Richard, Bill Doggett, Nina Simone, and Maynard Ferguson. According to Beamon, "they were all top-drawer attractions." His large shows at the City Auditorium were also diverse.

The top stars of 1956 featured an array of interracial talent, including Carl Perkins's "Blue Suede Shows," Al Hibbler, Frankie Lymon and the Teenagers, Chuck Berry, Shirley L. Lee, Della Reese, the Cleftones and Illinois Jacquet, Nat King Cole, June Christy, the 4 Freshman, and Ted Heath and his Bullish Orchestra—all of whom were backed by Beamon. Local acts were given big breaks by Beamon also. The Lloyd Terry Band, featuring a young high school vocalist named Gladys Knight, was given the opportunity to open for big acts at the Magnolia, performing for 30 minutes for $30. One night, according to lore, she begged Jackie Wilson to let her open for him and when she did, "she turned the place out." Beamon appears in the above photograph with Jackie Wilson (right, holding plaque) with emcee and disc jockey James "Alley Pat" Patrick (center). To the right, Beamon is pictured with the unforgettable James Brown.

This is a program booklet from Beaumon's Annual School Safety Patrol Benefit Show on May 1, 1952, featuring the Ravens, Percy Mayfield, Errol Garner, B.B. King, and hometown boy Chuck Willis.

This is a mobile advertisement board for Beamon's Community Chest Fund-Raiser at the City Auditorium, featuring the Orioles, Joe Liggins, and many others.

Over the years numerous persons worked for Beamon, including Annie Laurie Durrah, B.F. Cofer, Gerone Taylor, Roscoe Thomas, J. Russell Simmons, Marion Jackson, Roy Jones, Ken Knight, Rigdon Horton, Curtis Cosby, John Latimore, Maxine Phillips, A.C. Simmone, Jack Moore, Thomas Rogers, D.C. Usher, William Wright, John Williams, More Cain, and James Slacks. In 1976, Beamon joined the Atlanta Department of Corrections, where he managed the facility's food service department. He retired in 1996 and died on September 3, 1997.

Beamon and his partner, Herman Nash, purchased the Savoy Hotel in the Herndon Building in the 1950s. Auburn Avenue provided adequate and first-class lodging for African Americans who came to the city. From the Savoy to the Royal Hotel, rates were a $1 and up and meals were served at 6:30 a.m. and 10:00 a.m. Earlier, Mrs. James sold the Roosevelt Hotel in 1936 and moved to the West Side of Atlanta to Hunter Street, where she opened up the James Cafe. The hotel was sold and renamed after the famous New York ballroom, the Savoy. The renamed hotel was managed by Mrs. Charlie Mae Pearson and her husband.

Born in Albany, Georgia, Henry L. Wynn came to Atlanta in the late 1930s. Working as a bootblack, he possessed the desire to develop a business and obtained the space once occupied by Melvin Gaston's Silver Streak Grill on Auburn Avenue and Hilliard Street and opened Henry's Cabaret, featuring the Blue Room. (Courtesy of the Wynn family.)

Henry's Cabaret, located on the corner of Auburn Avenue and Hilliard Street, was later transformed to Henry's Stairway to the Stars, and featured top talent and cuisine. Some of the early acts at the Stairway to the Stars included exotic shake dancer Evelyn Moore, Jones Spencer, Grace Silver, and Bennie Stevens. The opening night band was the Jimmy Hensley band, which had come directly from the Minton Playhouse in New York. The vocalist was Clyde Terrell, billed as "the Golden Voice." (Courtesy of the Wynn family.)

Wynn later purchased the building at Auburn Avenue next to the Royal Peacock nightclub and then renovated and reopened Henry's Grill and Lounge at 180 Auburn Avenue, near the corner of Piedmont in 1948. The establishment featured musical entertainment by local singer Tommy Hines and his band. Lavishly decorated in blue, rose, and cream colors, the grill featured murals of the seasons. The grill opened with two chefs and offered steaks and chicken, as well as novelty items. Throughout his career, Mr. Wynn would own many businesses, including Champs Dry Cleaners, the Marietta Inn, Red Top Cab Company, H & H Liquor Store, Sparkle Car Wash, and two other clubs—Treasure Island and Morocco Lounge (formerly Club Poinciana). (Courtesy of the Wynn family.)

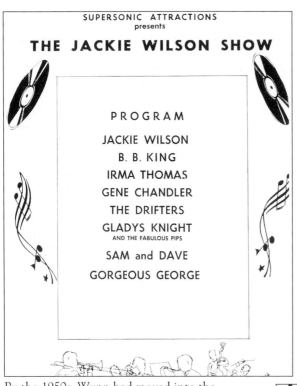

SUPERSONIC ATTRACTIONS
presents

THE JACKIE WILSON SHOW

PROGRAM

JACKIE WILSON

B. B. KING

IRMA THOMAS

GENE CHANDLER

THE DRIFTERS

GLADYS KNIGHT
AND THE FABULOUS PIPS

SAM and DAVE

GORGEOUS GEORGE

By the 1950s, Wynn had moved into the promotions business, creating Supersonic Attractions. The entertainment company sponsored some of the top acts in show business, including Lloyd "Mr. Personality" Price, shown here at right with Wynn. The nightclub also gave his stable of performers a space to perform. As a national promoter, Wynn showcased hundreds of artists. His cabaret of stars included Laverne Baker, James Brown, Gene Chandler, Ray Charles, Sam Cooke, Aretha Franklin, Gorgeous George, Roy Hamilton, Isaac Hayes, the Impressions, the Jackson Five, B.B. King, Ben E. King, Gladys Knight and the Pips, Major Lance, Patti Labelle and the Blue Bells, Jackie "Moms" Mabley, Pigmeat Markham, Otis Redding, Little Richard, Vibrations, Dionne Warwick, Spencer Wiggins, Jackie Wilson, and Stevie Wonder.

HENRY WYNN'S ENTERPRISES

TREASURE ISLAND
176 Auburn Avenue., N.E.

MOROCCO LOUNGE
145 Auburn Avenue, N.E.

RED TOP CAB CO. & SPARKLE CAR WASH
159 Auburn Avenue, N.E.

ROYAL PEACOCK SOCIAL CLUB, INC.
186½ Auburn Avenue, N.E.

HENRY'S GRILL & COCKTAIL LOUNGE
180 Auburn Avenue, N.E.

HENRY'S GRILL & LOUNGE—Miss Marice Carmichael, Manager
TREASURE ISLAND—Draft Beer & Country Style—Mrs. Edna Ray, Manager
MOROCCO LOUNGE—Mr. Joseph P. Foster, Manager
RED TOP CAB CO., INC., and SPARKLE CAR WASH—Mr. Jessie Bockley, Manager
MARIETTA INN and SUPER SONIC ATTRACTIONS, INC.
ROYAL PEACOCK SOCIAL CLUB, INC.—Mr. Velmon "Big Baby" Bolden
EASTER WEEK ATTRACTIONS—Hank Ballard and The Mid-Nighters—Saturday, Sunday, Monday, April 1, 2, 3
For Reservations CALL JA. 5-6986

HENRY WYNN'S ENTERPRISES
GROWING WITH ATLANTA

HENRY WYNN, President

ARTHUR M. PERRIN, Secretary

The Supersonic Lineup for one of Wynn's concerts included the Impressions, featuring Curtis Mayfield, now an Atlanta resident. Mayfield recalled coming to Atlanta and staying at the Old Forrest Arms Hotel during the late 1950s.

Following the death of Dr. Martin Luther King, Wynn organized one of the first entertainment tributes to him in 1971 at the City Auditorium, featuring Michael Jackson (seen here) and the Jackson Five and "Moms" Mabley. Wynn promoted shows until 1973, with one of his last shows featuring Marvin Gaye.

Pictured here is Diana Ross in the lobby of the Atlanta Civic Center, c. 1970s. Shortly after Martin Luther King's death, Motown Records sent its leading stars, including Miss Ross and the Supremes, Gladys Knight and the Pips, Stevie Wonder, and the Temptations, for a benefit concert which raised $25,000 for the Southern Christian Leadership Conference. Wynn's legacy was left with the numerous philanthropic organizations he so generously gave to, including the Butler Street YMCA, which received proceeds from many shows. Wynn was survived by his wife, Effie; daughters Henrietta and Claudia; and son, Henry Jr. The late Rev. Williams Holmes Borders eulogized Wynn as a "business genius who almost without academics operated with success eight businesses when most of us fail at one." (Courtesy of Bob Johnson.)

As a promoter, Wynn often had to go out of town, but while in town, his home was a haven for entertainers where he and his wife, Effie, often fed them home-cooked meals, according to daughter Claudia (left side of Jackie Wilson [center]). Claudia fondly remembered Jackie Wilson (seen here with the other members of his band), Mahalia Jackson, and Stevie Wonder eating dinner at their home during the 1950s and 1960s.

Four
The Bands and Musicians

Pictured here is Neal Montgomery's Combo, a favorite performing group for dances and parties, c. 1920s

The Elks Concert Band (seen here *c.* 1926) was one of several bands organized by Graham Jackson and Bill Shaw. Shaw had worked closely with Benjamin Davis, publisher of the *Atlanta Independent*. He became one of the first African-American booking agents in Atlanta, securing acts for the Roof Garden. Many of these bands got their break at the 81 Theater under the direction of Eddie Heywood Sr. Heywood was directing the pit band when a young musician named Graham Jackson came to Atlanta right out of high school as the director of a traveling band. So impressed was the management that they offered him a job to take over the house orchestra and play the new organ the theater was installing.

There were numerous African-American bands in Atlanta from the 1920s to the 1940s, including the Cosmopolitan Orchestra, the Collegiate Ramblers, Hassie L. Domineck's Ambassadors, R.L. Baugh Dukes of Rhythm, the Troubadours, DeCoates and his Orchestra, Waymond Brown Cavaliers, Jimmy Lott and his Merrimakers, Kid Miller and the Marietta Orchestra, Rudy Brown Serenaders, J.S. Hayes and the Three Notes, Herman Scott and his Orchestra, Raymond Taylor and his Rhythm Boys, Willie Rogers and his Orchestra, Billy Valentine, Billy De Lyons, the Capitol City Orchestra, and the Dokey Band, one of the oldest bands in Atlanta. According to William Coates, it was a dance band that played under the direction of P.S. "Pop" Cooke (seen here), a native of Cobb County, Georgia. Cooke served as secretary, treasurer, and business agent for the Atlanta Musicians Protective Association, also known as Atlanta Local 462.

The Collegiate Ramblers entertained black Atlantans during the 1920s. The band featured Neal Montgomery and Wayman Carver (third from right).

At Booker T. Washington High School, the first public high school for African Americans in Atlanta and built in 1924, a group of students organized the Rambling Preps; they are, from left to right, as follows: Clarence Brown, Robert Craddock, Neal James, James Jackson, Sam Cochran, William Coates, and Emmit King. (Reprinted from the Washingtonian Yearbook.)

Many of the members of the Rambling Preps would have a long and memorable career in the field of music and entertainment. One member of the Rambling Preps was Samuel W. Cochran, who lived in the Summerhill community and graduated from Washington High School. Despite his physical handicap due to infantile paralysis, Cochran was a talented pianist who won many amateur contests. Cochran played with Tiny Bradshaw and Erskine Hawkins and led his own band for 20 years. He also repaired and tuned pianos.

Ralph Mays had a long career as a musician. He led the Troubadours at the Sunset and also managed the club. Mays was also employed by the Atlanta Public Schools.

Another member, William Coates, was born in Atlanta and raised in the Summerhill neighborhood. He learned to play his instrument at the Summerhill School, later renamed E.P. Johnson. J. Neal Montgomery, who would later have his own band and bring major acts to Atlanta, lived near Coates as a child. Coates would sit on the curb and listen to Montgomery play. Coates made a deal with the Cohen Music Store on Broad Street and paid $1 down and $1 a week and walked home with a C-melody Saxophone.

Two talented drummers were Lawrence Walker and Lafayette Lawson (seen here). Lawson attended Washington High School and the University of Chicago Music School and played for Billie Holiday, Dinah Washington, Nina Simone, and others. He died in 1986. Lawrence Earl Walker, the drummer for the Billy De Lyons Troubadours, organized his band in 1939. The band included Albert Holley on guitar, George Adams on trumpet, Rufus Tucker, Austell Allen, Stanford Hinton, Joseph Harris, and Ralph Mays. Their theme melody was "Drums of Joy." Another band he played in included the Billy Valentine Trio, which was formed in 1947 and consisted of Charles Holloway, Q.P. Jones, and Wesley Jackson.

By the 1940s, the sound of swing music had ushered in a new era in band performances in Atlanta, offering a great opportunity for bands to compete with one another as was often the case at many of the night spots. The Sunset Casino began to offer dances after Saturday night football games. Ralph Mays, a native of Forsyth, Georgia, found himself at the Sunset as the band leader for the Troubadours and also the house manager. He also played regularly at the Top Hat Club with Sammy Green's "Hot Harlem Review." From left to right are, these musicians are as follows: (front row) Waymon Carver, Horace Scott, Herman Scott, Robert Shropshire (drums), and William Fowlkes (piano); (back row) Jimmy Lott (only partially shown), John Peek, and Rudy Brown (bass).

William "Bill" DeLyons Thomas (front left) and his Troubadours are pictured at the Sunset Casino, c. 1930s. From left to right are as follows: (front row) McGhee, George Adams, Paul Kendall, unidentified, Neal James, Rufus Tucker, and unidentified; (back row) Will "Cab" Hall (vocalist nicknamed "Cab" because he sounded like Cab Calloway), Didi Dozier, Lawrence Walker (drummer), "Specks" (guitar), and Joe Thomas (bass). Seated to the right in front is Duke Ellington. (Courtesy of Ralph Mays.)

Members of the Red McAllister Band, *c.* 1940s, are pictured on the Top Hat Club stage. From left to right, they are as follows: Hillard Foster, Mason "Spooks" Johnson, Lewis Phillip, Sam "Porky" Slaughter, and unidentified.

Following in the musical footsteps of his father (seen here) as a member of the pit band of the 81 Theater was Eddie Heywood Jr., who became one of the most popular jazz musicians in the country. Eddie Sr. was born in Sumter, South Carolina, son of a minister who loved music. He attended the Boston Conservatory before coming to Atlanta. He began playing and directing the pit for the stage revues, with his son soon joining him. Heywood, Sr. recorded several songs, including "Pawn Shop Blues" and "Chasing the Cats." He died on April 2, 1942. Eddie Jr. graduated from Booker T. Washington High School and moved to New Orleans, Kansas City, Missouri, and Texas working with the Clarence Love Orchestra. (Courtesy of Lottie Heywood Watkins.)

For the next ten years, Heywood performed throughout the country until 1931, when he found himself the pianist for the Benny Carter band. It was with Carter that Heywood met Billie Holiday. She was so impressed with his work that she insisted on having him arrange for her as well as accompany her on several recording dates.

Later, he became the house pianist at the Village Vanguard. This stint would introduce him to some of the most recognized talent of the period. John Hammond, who had already helped to nurture the careers of Count Basie, Billie Holiday, and Benny Goodman, urged Eddie to organize a sextet that included trumpeter Doc Cheatham and trombonist Vic Dickenson.

From 1943 to 1947, the sextet rode a wave of popularity and was heard on radio records. He arranged music for Bing Crosby, which escalated his popularity once the records were released. He began to make a cross-country tour from New York to Hollywood, and stopped in his old hometown of Atlanta and performed at the Top Hat Club and the City Auditorium.

His arrangement of Cole Porter's "Begin with Beguine" brought him even greater fame. Cole Porter once remarked that "he wished he had written it the way Heywood arranged it." Following a temporary paralysis of his hands and its therapy, Heywood came back and wrote three hit tunes: "Land of Dreams," "Soft Summer Breeze," and his biggest hit, "Canadian Sunset." Eddie Heywood Jr. died at age 73 in December 1988.

The Stardusters Band grew out of the Booker T. Washington High School Follies when Elmer Calloway, brother of Cab Calloway, encouraged Lloyd Terry to organize a group. The band was very popular with the high school set, playing at many of the YMCA dances and canteens in the 1950s. Members of the Stardusters are, from left to right, as follows: Lloyd Terry, Harold Elder (trumpet), Edward Emory (saxophone), Mac Smith, Harold Randolph (drums), and Bill Odum (piano). William "Bill" Odum was a native of Atlanta and a graduate of Morehouse College. His musical group was and still is one of the most popular combos in the city. Lloyd Terry went on to Clark College, and studied under Professor Waymon Carver. (Courtesy of Lloyd Terry.)

George "Kid" Miller, a native of Kennesaw, Georgia, had a trio of musicians that was a local favorite for parties and dances. He played at Dobbins Air Force Base for many years. (Courtesy of Digging It Up Archives.)

Cleveland Lyons (seen here), along with Bill Doggett, helped to popularize the organ sound in rhythm and blues music. (Courtesy of Emma Lyons Hardnett.)

Cleveland Lyons was a wonderful organist. Lyons and his band, the Cleve Lyons Combo, played all over the country and backed up such stars as the Pips, Tommy Brown, Little Clarence, and Grover Mitchell. Lyons died on August 21, 1962, when he shot himself. He was eulogized at Ebenezer Baptist Church by his friend Rev. Dr. Martin Luther King, who said, "Lyons's music caressed the heart like a symphony of the sun. His music was like the warmth of the spring." After his death, the remaining band members formed the Master's Combo. Pictured are, from left to right, the following: Paul Mitchell, John Peek, Harold Grissom, James "Dub" Hudson, John T. Kelley, Elmer Lewis, and Carolyn Jeter, who worked with the combo's public relations. (Reprinted from the *Atlanta Voice*.)

John Peek (trumpet) and Winton Kelley (piano) play at a jam session, c. 1950. Peek played with the Lucky Millander Orchestra and the Cleveland Lyons Band and then led the Master's Combo. He currently directs the African-American Symphony in Atlanta and is one of the most respected arrangers, composers, and musicians in the city. (Courtesy of Clarence Hubbard.)

This Sunday afternoon jam session featured, from left to right, the following: Lafayette Lawson (drums), Duke Pearson (trumpet), Donald Edwards (trumpet), and unidentified.

Atlanta was the birthplace of two great female pianists and composers. Mary Lou Williams, born in 1910, played with Duke Ellington's Washingtonians and the Andy Kirk Band. Cornelia "Connie" Berry (seen here), known as the "Queen of the Ivory," was born in Atlanta in 1904 and graduated from Clark College. By the 1920s and 1930s, she traveled extensively across the country playing for cafe society in New York and Hollywood, California. She performed at Harlem's Club Ubangi and Club Onyx and briefly had a New York radio show called *The Sophisticated Lady of Song*. She recorded for Brunswick Records. Miss Berry played with Tommy Dorsey and Duke Ellington and performed for President Franklin Delano Roosevelt often at his home in Warm Springs, Georgia. Connie Berry died in 1995. (Courtesy of Ralph Mays.)

Pictured at the Waluhaje, c. 1960s, are, from left to right, the following: Jimmy Whittington (on the mike); (front row) David Hudson, John McCaldy, James Hudson, James Patterson, and Elmer Lewis; (back row) Thomas Howard, Marion Booker, Milton Clarke, Wilson Bostic, Mason Johnson, unidentified, and Duke Pearson. (Courtesy of Clarence Hubbard.)

One of the greatest blues musicians to come out of Atlanta was Willie "Piano Red" Perryman. He was born in 1913 in Hamilton, Georgia, one of nine children born to sharecropping parents. In 1919, his family moved to Atlanta, and he began playing rent and house parties and fish fries in Atlanta's Summerhill community with his brother Rufus, also a musician, who was known as "Speckled Red." Perryman began to play at the local clubs. He recorded "Rocking With Red" and "You Got the Right String Baby, but the Wrong Yo-Yo" with his six-piece band called the Interns. Perryman had a large white following that was further enhanced by his gigs at Underground Atlanta. He died in July 1985.

James "Put" Jackson (seen here playing drums) was born in Madison, Georgia, and grew up in Atlanta and joined the Rambling Preps at Washington High School. He later attended Morris Brown College and had a distinguished career in entertainment, playing with Graham Jackson and Neal Montgomery. Of interest, when he was young, Jackson had to lie to his mother to get out at night to play at the nightclubs. (Courtesy of Linda Jackson.)

Tim Arkansas, a native of the Summerhill section of Atlanta, performed on the Snooky Lanson show in 1962. He recorded an album on historic Summerhill, including a song "Hell Raisers of Summerhill." Inspired by Josh White, a famous folk singer, Arkansas broke ground, appearing at such clubs as the TIKI and the Morroco Lounge with his innovative brand of folk music. (Courtesy of Digging It Archives.)

Marion Brown (left), a jazz saxophonist, was a native of Atlanta who received his musical education from Howard and Wesleyan Universities. He left college to record with John Coltrane and later formed his own group, traveling to Europe. One of his works included "Afternoon of a Georgia Faun."

Graham Jackson plays accordion with a group of seasoned Atlanta musicians, c. 1960s.

The Hudson Brothers consisted of brothers David and James, both born in Gwinnett County and educated at David T. Howard High School and Clark College. David played with such musicians as Ernie Fields, Sonny Stitt, and the Jewel Tucker Band. He also had a band called Little David and the Twisters, which performed at many of the white clubs in Atlanta. After a stint in the army, James played with jazz pianist Tommy Flanigan and backed up many of the local singers and Cleveland Lyons. Both brothers were schoolteachers in Atlanta.

Left: Saxophonist Fred "Buck" Jackson, a native of Chattanooga, Tennessee, attended Washington High School and Morris Brown College. He played with Lil Green, Chuck Willis, Paul Gayten, Lloyd Price, and Lionel Hampton, as well as his own band, the Modern Jazz Septet.

Right: Saxophonist Walter "Billy" Reid was a native of Atlanta and a graduate of Washington High School and Clark College. He was for many years a member of the Stardusters and the Lloyd Terry Band.

James Patterson (center), though born in Kingston, Georgia, came to Atlanta as a baby. Both of his parents were musically talented, with his mother playing the piano and his father performing with a minstrel group. He began playing piano at the age of six, learned several other musical instruments like the saxophone and flute, and furthered his musical interest at Washington and Turner High Schools. A music major at Clark College, Patterson was influenced by Waymon Carver. He played and backed up many singers, including James Brown.

Top left: Duke Pearson was born Columbus Calvin Pearson in 1932 in the Summerhill section of Atlanta. He was nicknamed "Duke" by an uncle who admired Duke Ellington's music. He studied piano and brass instruments. Pearson toured with Donald Byrd and Nancy Wilson and worked as producer for Blue Note Records from 1963 to 1970. He later toured with Carmen McRae and Joe Williams in the 1970s. He developed multiple sclerosis, which prevented him from playing further and died on August 4, 1980.

Top right: Shown here are "Jayno" Wright on flute and Junior Harris on bass.

Bottom: Jewel Tucker was a talented pianist, bassist, and trumpeter. Born in 1931 in Atlanta, he moved to Detroit and attended Cass High School, learning how to play trumpet and then piano. He traveled the carnival circuit with Sammy Green and Irvin C. Miller and then returned to Atlanta, where he graduated from Washington High School. After a stint in the army, he played for the bands of Chuck Willis, Percy Mayfield, and Big Jay McNeely and performed with Ruth Brown, Della Reese, Sonny Stitt, and many others. In 1965, he began plans to write a book, *Who's Who Among Atlanta Musicians.* (Photographs on this page courtesy of Clarence Hubbard.)

Horace Silver is seen here wailing away on his piano. (Courtesy of Clarence Hubbard)

There were many great saxophonists in Atlanta; one of the most popular of these musicians was Edwin Driskell (seen here). Driskell, born in Jacksonville, Florida, came to Atlanta in 1924 to attend high school at Morehouse College. His mother was born in Atlanta and played the piano, along with his sister and brother. Driskell started out on the trombone, but his mother bought him a saxophone. When he arrived in Atlanta, Driskell joined the music scene, playing at afternoon hops and fraternity dances. He played at the 81 Theater with Eddie Heywood, the 91, and the Grand Theater on Decatur Street, earning from $1 an hour to $6 a night, when he played for some white groups. Often Driskell and other musicians would play at Rush Week dances at Georgia Tech. Driskell recalled playing with some of the early African-American musicians of the late twenties like "Dick" Finley, Pete Clark, Nelson Jackson (tenor sax), Harper Douglas (banjo), Harold Whittington (trumpet), and George Derricotte (saxophone). Driskell's last professional appearance was in 1953 with Cleveland Lyons at a nightclub on Juniper and Ponce De Leon. Driskell became employed with the post office in 1941 and worked there for over 20 years.

Five
The Singers

Atlanta could boast some of the most talented singers in the country. Not to be forgotten are Bill Bailey, who left Atlanta to perform with the Count Basie band; Katherine "Hoody" McCool, who performed with jazz and blues entertainers such as Ida Cox, Sammy Green, and Leon Claxton; Billy Wright; and local musicians Red McAllister and Austell Allen. Others included Annie Laurie, Clyde Terrell, Elaine Dudley, Dodd Hicks, Richard "Blues" Gibbs, Little Sonny, Liz Lands, Lee Moses, Louise Freeman, "Little" Helen Thompson, Juanita High, Joann Glass, Eddie Sawyer, Gloria Meadows, Sandra Hall, Barbara Hall, Freddy Terrell, Little Ella, Lynn Westbrooks, Dave Whitfield, and hundreds others. There were also hundreds of singing groups. Though many never branched beyond the "chitterling circuit" of the South, there were several from Atlanta and Georgia who went on to achieve national acclaim—for example, Big Maybelle, Little Richard, James Brown, Billy Wright, Chuck Willis, Gladys Knight, and Arthur Conley. The 1970s ushered in a new decade of powerful vocalists, including Liz Spaggus and Theresa Hightower.

Little Richard called Billy Wright, known for his colorful clothing, matching shoes, pompadour hairdo, and his make-up Pancake 31, "the most fantastic entertainer he had ever seen." Born William Wright on May 23, 1918, in Atlanta, "Billy" began singing as a child at the Mt. Vernon Baptist Church. During the early 1930s, he began performing with Andrew Fairchild at the 81 Theater. Between 1949 and 1951, Billy Wright had four top-ten rhythm and blues hits. Some of his hits included "Keep Your Hand on Your Heart and Your Mind on Me" and "Blues for My Baby." According to Little Richard, it was Wright who helped him get his first break when he introduced him to a white disc jockey, Zenas Sears. (Courtesy of Digging It Up Archives.)

Little Richard, the 18-year-old native of Macon,Georgia, was still traveling with legendary vaudeville star Spencer "Snake" Anthony and his revue when his first recording session took place at WGST. He was backed by Billy Wright's band. The session produced a local hit titled, "Every Hour," which was played on WERD. Little Richard played every club in Atlanta. He is shown between sets at the Royal Peacock in the 1960s. (Courtesy of Count Jackson.)

Before Keith Sweat, there was Tommy Brown, known for his weeping and crying antics. (Courtesy of Edward Emory.)

Julius and Donald High (seen here), graduated from David T. Howard High School. Donald began performing with the Cleveland Lyons Band and later formed a quartet while at Clark College, "the College Four." His first recording was "Peep Around Your Own Backdoor." His brother, Julius, who took the stage name "Lotsa Popa," began singing with a group called the Twighlighters, and they played the high school circuit. A local and regional favorite, Lotsa Poppa is still performing regularly. (Courtesy of Digging It Up Archives.)

Born Harold "Chuck" Willis on January 31, 1928, in Atlanta, Willis grew up near the Bell Street area. By the late 1940s, Willis was performing the floorshows of the Club Zanzibar and singing vocals with the Red McAllister and Roy Mays band. He was very popular at the teenage canteens sponsored by the YMCA. Willis was a local celebrity until Zenas "Daddy" Sears began to showcase him at talent shows. Sears eventually became manager for Willis and helped him to get a weekly television show and introduced him to an executive at Columbia Records, recording several tunes including "Can't You See." In 1952, he wrote "My Story," which shot all the way to number two on the Billboard "Juke Box" Rhythm and Blues list for two weeks. Willis died tragically at the age of 30 in April 1958. (Courtesy of Clarence Hubbard.)

Zilla Florine Mays Hinton was known as Atlanta's "Dream Girl." Her brothers Cleveland and Roy Mays were well-known trumpeters on the music scene. Zilla performed in many night spots, including the Club Poinciana and the Waluhaje. Legend has it that one evening at Club Poinciana, Zilla bumped into Dinah Washington, who had heard of this phenomenal voice and said, "So this is the !≠$& whose trying to take my place." Dinah was known for her candor, but Zilla was known for her powerful voice. She married popular blues singer and recording star J. Lewis Hinton. Zilla made the transformation to gospel music and hosted the morning gospel show on WAOK Radio Station until her death on September 11, 1995.

Two of Atlanta's famous female vocalists of the 1960s were "Miss Tulip" (left) and Lil Saddler (right), seen along with other musicians at a jam session. (Courtesy of Clarence Hubbard.)

Here are the popular Atlanta vocalists Gladys Knight and the Pips in their heyday.

Born in 1944, Gladys Knight came from a musical family. Both of her parents, Mr. and Mrs. Merald (Elizabeth) Knight, sang with the Wings over Jordan choir. At the age of four, Gladys made her first public appearance singing at Mt. Moriah Baptist Church. She appeared on the Old Gold Original Amateur Hour and won the title of National Radio Champion. She won the Ted Mack Amateur Hour in 1951, taking home a gold cup and $2,000. From 1950 to 1953, Gladys toured with the Morris Brown College choir. The Pips, including her cousin Eleanor O. Guest, were organized during a family gathering. (Courtesy of William Guest, Gladys, Edward Patton, and Merald Knight.)

In 1962, the Tams hooked up with musical publisher Bill Lowery, who ultimately became their manager. In Rick Hall's Fame Studio in Muscle Shoals, Alabama, they recorded such records as "Untie Me" and "What Kind of Fool."

Born in Dawson, Georgia, Otis Redding was a household word in Atlanta, having gotten his feet wet at the Lithonia Country Club in Dekalb County and performing with the group Johnny Jenkins and the Pinetoppers at the Royal Peacock in Atlanta. He rapidly grew in fame and recorded several albums. He died on December 10, 1967, at the age of 26, along with the members of his band, the Bar Kays, when his plane crashed in Lake Mononoa in Wisconsin. His death greatly affected many Atlantans, especially singer Arthur Conley, Redding's protege.

Six

Dancers, Masters of Ceremonies, Comedians, and Radio Stations

The art of dancing had reached climactic proportions on Atlanta's stage when the popular Nicholas Brothers (above, right) opened for Dizzy Gillespie at the City Auditorium on August 2, 1945. Local dancers such as Top and Bottom (above, left) opened for many of the entertainers and performed many of the floorshows at the nightclubs. Atlanta could claim a bevy of dancers, from burlesque to tap to creative and jazz. During the 1930s, one of the noted dancers was Little Willie Mae Smith, who left Atlanta to work in the movies. She appeared in the movie *The Exile*, one of Oscar Micheaux's "all-colored" cast pictures. Another dancer was known as Baby Cox, who performed in Harlem in the 1930s at Connie's Inn and other places. (Courtesy of Digging It Up Archives.)

This unidentified dancer is doing her thing on stage, *c.* 1950. Dancers usually opened up shows or performed between sets.

Dancers Clarence Hubbard and Mildred Jenkins perform a Calypso/Caribbean number on the stage of the Magnolia Ballroom. Hubbard was one of the most popular dancers, jazz enthusiasts, and record collectors in Atlanta. During the 1950s and 1960s, he photographed many of the events and personalities of the entertainment scene in Atlanta. (Courtesy of Clarence Hubbard.)

One of the most popular dancers during the 1940s was Ruby Calhoun (top left), who is shown in one of her "bump and grind" poses at the Elks Club. The dance due Flash and Dash (seen top right) were popular performers in Harlem on Broadway. "Flash," or James Banner, was a native of Atlanta, and "Dash" was the nephew of movie star Stepin Fetchit. Rosita "Chicken" Lockhart (right) popularized the exotic "Chicken" dance with her feather boa and gyrating moves. She was also known as the "Ninth Wonder of the World."

Atlantans first saw Ray Sneed Jr. in the Katherine Dunham dance sequence in the MGM musical *Stormy Weather*, starring Lena Horne in 1943. He also performed in the movie *Jivin in Be-Bop*, featuring Dizzy Gillespie. Sneed came to Atlanta during the 1940s and worked as the ballet master at the Oglethorpe School. His training in dance came from the American School for Ballet. Sneed danced at most of the popular nightclubs throughout the country. Adored by Eleanor Roosevelt, who liked his "Ole Man River," Mary McCleod Bethune, and boxer Joe Louis, who liked his rendition of "Nobody Knows the Trouble I've Seen," Sneed was one of the most versatile and talented dancers in the country. (Courtesy of Mrs. Leola Gartrell.)

Some of the other numerous Atlanta dancers included John Scruggs, Markee (the exotic dancer), Billie Booker, Clay Bradley, Clyde Terrell, Ruby Calhoun, Mabel Lee, Queenie Davis, Von and Gertrude, Ella, Snooks and Allen (exotic dancers), Madame Kilroy, Nikkie and Rikkie, and Flash and Dash. In this picture, an unidentified dancer is pictured with vocalist Jimmy Witherspoon, c. 1950. One dancer (not pictured) worked as a manicurist at the University Barber Shop near the Atlanta University Center and was a regular at Paschal's Restaurant, greeting everybody with "Darling." However, in her heyday, she was billed as Lady Tanya and shared the spotlight with many greats on the stages of the Small Paradise, the Baby Grand in New York, and Club Poinciana and the Royal Peacock on Auburn Avenue. (Courtesy of Harmon Perry.)

Stand-up comedians evolved from the early days of vaudeville. Atlanta produced many local and nationally known African-American comics, including Claude Dickerson (shown here), known as "Tiny," a comic who performed with circuses, including the Silas Green from New Orleans revue. He died in 1948 in Atlanta, which he had adopted as his hometown. Another comic, Nipsy Russell, according to Old Fourth Ward residents, used to wear knickerbocker pants when performing in front of the 81 Theater on Decatur Street. Other comics were Clay Tyson, a native of Atlanta and a graduate of David T. Howard High School who like so many others also began his career at the 81 Theater. He left Atlanta in 1949 to pursue his professional career, returning to Atlanta to perform at the Royal Peacock. Tiny Dixon, another comic, was managed by Red McAllister, Porky Slaughter, and Al Jackson.

119

Opening the show was an important part of the production. In addition to radio personalties serving as emcees, Atlanta claimed several well-known masters of ceremonies, including Baron L. Wilson, Gip Sandman Robert, Odell "Gorgeous" George, and Bill Murray (below). Gorgeous George (left) is seen here with his processed hairdo, which was popularized in the early 1960s.

With the advent of radio, much of the music of the decade could be heard over the airwaves, along with the voices of radio personalities. Radio played an important and vital part in the growth and development of the popularity of music. Several white-owned radio stations operated in Atlanta, including WEAS and WBGE, which occasionally featured African-American talent over the air. Pictured here (c. 1940) are, from left to right, as follows: Dave Bondu, B.B. Beamon, and Ned Lukens, also known as "the Bellboy," on the air of WEAS.

The history of African-American radio in Atlanta can be traced to two people: Jesse Blayton, founder of WERD, and Zenas Sears, who helped to bring black radio into the mainstream of black listeners when he established WAOK. After a serving in the Army, Sears returned to work at the station WATL. No station in Atlanta was playing music by black musicians and singers at the time. Sears (seated in front of the microphone) is shown with bandleader Austell Allen (seated, right) and members of his band, including Tippin Hawk (standing, center), the vocalist for the group, c. 1940. Allen, along with Graham Jackson and Sam Cochran, was credited with introducing the organ to jazz music.

Many of the radio personalities often hosted the shows and concerts at the local nightclubs. One such disk jockey was James "Alley Pat" Patrick, a native of Montezuma, Georgia, and son of a Baptist preacher and nurse. In 1931, his family moved to Atlanta and settled on Hilliard Street. Patrick graduated from Booker T. Washington High School and Morehouse College. One night while calling Bingo at the Lincoln Country Club and "jiving" over the loud speakers, Ken Knight, the program director of WERD invited him to do a voice tape, and he was soon on the air for WERD. He later joined WAOK, the first 24-hour station with an African-American music format.

Before his stint as the singing disc jockey for WERD, Herb Lance was an accomplished singer and vocalist who performed with Duke Ellington and Dizzy Gillespie. Lance recorded several songs, including "My Buddy" and "Close Your Eyes." He also owned the Crisis Recording Company and was a jazz promoter and had a show called the *Purple Grotto Jazz Show*. Lance was known as Cousin Herb Lance. He wrote the lyrics to Ruth Brown's popular hit "Mama He Treats Your Daughter Mean."

Other "on air" personalities and employees of the station who would come later for WERD were Graham Jackson; Ned Lukens; Bob Brisendane; William Boyd; Raphel McIver; Billie Geter Thomas (seen here), who provided the WERD Theater presentations; Roosevelt Johnson, who was the first African-American disk jockey for WBGE; Robert Scott, a graduate of the Cambridge School of Radio and Television who had a career in radio in New York and New Jersey before coming to Atlanta; and Preston Mobley, who had worked at WBGE and WAKE while a student at Clark College. These were the pioneers of radio in Atlanta during the 1950s and 1960s.

Shown here is a great assembly of talent. They are, from left to right, as follows: (front row) Jack Gibson and Ray McIver; (back row) John Peek, Duke Pearson, unidentified, and Waymon Carver, c. 1950s. Most folks recognized the name Jack "the Rapper" Gibson because of its association with the popular convention known as "A Family Affair," which provided opportunities for persons trying to break into the recording industries and be discovered, as well as popular recording stars who wanted to share their secrets of the business. However, to many Atlantans, he will always be known as "Jockey Jack," the popular radio personality for WERD, emcee for many of the shows at the nightclubs, and pioneer in radio and entertainment. (Courtesy of Harmon Perry.)

Duke Pearson (center, behind piano) and other musicians jam before the WERD mike. (Courtesy of Clarence Hubbard.)

In 1954, Zenas Sears acquired WAOK and created a stellar lineup of radio personalities which included C. Allen Redd for the *Message Program*, Zilla Mays Hinton for the *Mysterious Dream Girl*, and Willie "Piano Red" Perryman, who had the *Dr. Feelgood Show*. Janice Johnson, James "Jim" Wood, Harrison Smith, and Esmond Patterson were gospel disc jockeys, and other radio personalities included Ed "Nassau Daddy" Cook; Frankie Harp; Burke "Thin Man" Johnson, who later wrote a record column for the *Atlanta Voice*; and Jerry Thompson. Shown here is a show announcement for the WAOK 11th Anniversary Concert in 1965.

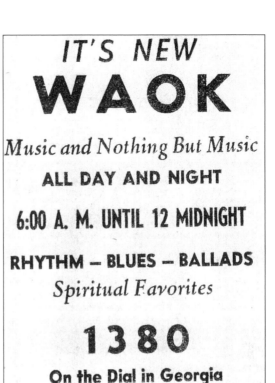

Record stores were important for local and national artists to get their recordings in the homes of their fans. There were several shops owned by African Americans in Atlanta, including the Luden and Bates on North Pryor, and Worthy's Place on Auburn Avenue during the 1920s. By the 1940s and 1950s, there was Buddy's Toyland on Mitchell Street, Smith's Music and Appliance, Auburn Avenue Record Shop, and the Butler Street Hi-Fi Record Center, owned by Lafayette Lawson and Robert Wilson. Opening in the 1960s was the Music Inn, owned by Shelby Welch, with the popular Hugh "Boo Boo" Wyatt, and Prelude Record Shop owned by Carolyn Geter and Herman Johnson. Cleopas Johnson established Johnson's Music Store on Hunter Street.

125

Epilogue

Atlanta has boasted some of the most talented musicians and entertainers in the country. During the 1960s, Jewel Tucker and Clarence Hubbard compiled biographies of most of these persons. I know that I have omitted some names that deserved to be recognized, but due to space, many of the musicians could not be featured in this publication. Some of them are listed below, with much gratitude for their contribution to the entertainment industry in Atlanta:

George (Alif Lamed) Adams, Isaiah "Ike" Alexander, Austell Allen, Herman L. "Spider" Allen, Tim Arkansas, Harold Banks, Robert Barber, George Battle, Grady Bennett, Rudolph Bess, Don Biggs, James A. "Jack" Blackwell, Hamilton Bohannon, Marion Booker Jr., Gordon Boykins, Frank A. Bray, William J. Braynon, Clarence Brown, J.S. Brown, Henry Bryant, John Buck, Rodney Buruss, Jimmy Calhoun, John Calhoun, Doug Carn, Clarence Chandler, John Churchfield, Arthur Clark, Donald Clarke, Milton Clarke, Peter Clark, Richard Clark, William Coates, Samuel W. Cochran, Ben Cofer, Otis H. Collier, Lamar Collins, Percy H. Conley, Walter L. Cook, Aaron Cooke, Robert Corbin, Edward "Jo-Jo" Cox, Fred Cox Sr. and Jr., Waymon "Pee-Wee" Dabney, Rick Davis, Russell Davis, Curell DeLoan, George Dericotte, Rabbi Dixon, Albert Dobbins, H.L. Domineck, Donnell Edwards, Harold Elder, Edward Emory, Frederick D. Evans, Otis Finch, William Thomas Finley, Edward Florence, John H. Floyd, Eddie Lee Foster, Hillard G. Foster, Nathaniel Foster, Nylas Foster, Billy Freeman, Ronald Hampton, Charlie Harding, George Harper, Willie Harper, James Harris, Joe Harris, Arthur Hawkins, Frank Hawkins, Charles Holloway, Calvin Howard, Charles Howard, Thomas Howard, David Hudson, James Hudson, Eugene Gaines, James "Skeet" Gaines, Jay Gholson, Thomas Goodwin, Franklin Gordon, Lewis Grant, William "Gorilla" Green, Richard H. Grissom, Coleman Jackson, Edward M. Jackson, Fred G. "Buck" Jackson, Grady "Fats" Jackson, James "Cha-Cha" Jackson, James Clint Jackson, Laymon A. Jackson, Robert L. Jackson, Roy W. Jackson, Wesley Jackson, Neal James, Reese James, William Jefferson, Curtis Jenkins, Cleopas R. Johnson, Leroy Johnson, Mason Johnson, Roy Lee Johnson, Edward "Buzzy" Jones, George Jones, Jesse J. Jones, John Wesley Jones, Morris Jones, Bobby Keith, John T. Kelley, Cornelius King, James E. King, Tommy Lagon, Lafayette Lawson, John Lee, Aldolphus Lester, Elmer Lewis, Foster Lewis, Alexander B. Lockhart, John Lockhart, James L. Lott, Marcellus Lowe, Leroy "Floyd Thunder" Lukes, Clyde W. Lynn, E.B. Matthews, James J. "Jive Boy" Matthews, Ralph Mays, Roy Mays, William C. McClendon, Walter McCombs, Joseph McGahee, Rufus Middlebrooks, Frank Miller, George Miller, Winfred Mills, Paul F. Mitchell, James E. "Hank" Moore, Vincent Lee Moses, Allen Thomas Murphy, Marvin "Duck" Neal, James G. Newman, Gunzell Norah, William "Bill" Odum, Virginia Owens, David Parker, James Patterson, Thomas Patton, John Peek, Columbus "Duke" Pearson, Ernest L.H. Pepper, Willie "Piano Red" Perryman, Lloyd Phinazee, John W. Poindexter, Horace "Red" Prayer, Paul Randle, Walter "Billy" Reid, Leon Reynolds, Bobby Ringfield, Frederick G. Robinson, Woodie Rogers, Thomas H. Ross, Horace W. "Wimp" Scott, Julius Shaw, William Shorter, J.W. Simpson, William Sims, Curtis Smith, Jerry Lee Smith, Johnny B. Smith, Marion Smith, McClellan Smith, Richard "Smitty" Smith, William Smith, Willie Joe Smith, James "Bro. Jennings" Speer, Edward Spence, Robert L. Stevens, Darwin Strickland, Frank L. Stubbs, Andrew A. Tabb, Alonzo Taylor, Charles Terrell, Lloyd Terry, Joseph Thomas, Eddie Tigner, James Tigner, Jewel Tucker, Rufus Tucker, Bobby Tuggle, Eugene Turner, Lawrence Walker, Cosby Wallace, Ernest Wallace, Erwin Wallace, Borah Walton, Joel R. Ward, William C. Ward, Rudy Welmaker, Billy Whetstone, David Whitfield, Dan Whitner, James Wiggins, James Willis, Willie J. "Pete" Willis, Julius Wimby, Marvin Wimby, Arnold Worthen, Alfred D. Wyatt, and William W. Zackery.

Acknowledgments

How does one begin to thank those individuals who made this book possible? It seems that each project that I undertake is a relative of a previous one. And so it is the same with this book, *African-American Entertainment in Atlanta*.

During the researching phase for my first exhibit and publication, *Hidden Treasures* in 1989, I discovered some wonderful images of the entertainment life of African Americans in Atlanta from photographers such as Griff Davis and Harmon Perry. But it was a photograph of a group of musicians at the turn of the century taken by Atlanta's first African-American photographer, Thomas Askew, that really garnered my attention. The musicians included his sons and a neighbor. The photo was in the possession of Isaiah Blocker, the grandson of Askew who was now living in California. It confirmed that we were musically talented and that we sought to entertain and to be entertained even before the turn of the century.

Through years of researching the *Atlanta Independent* and the *Atlanta Daily World* newspapers, I uncovered a subject that had not been written and documented in book form. I said that I would attempt it. However, I was pleasantly interrupted by the opportunity to publish *Going Against the Wind: A Pictorial History of African-Americans in Atlanta*. The results of that book made it easier for me to resume my journey down the night life scene of Atlanta, behind the scenes of clubs and halls into the world of those who would entertain us—musicians, dancers, singers, comedians, and promoters.

Lastly, a meeting with Clarence Hubbard, a jazz bibliophile, record collector, photographer, and outstanding dancer, made it necessary to finish this book. My meeting with him in front of his apartment was overwhelming. Hubbard pulled out images of practically every local musician in Atlanta and some of the big stars that performed here, such as Billie Holiday, Ruth Brown, and my favorite, Dinah Washington. The most important aspect of that meeting was a stack of faded sheets of paper with biographical sketches of Atlanta musicians. I am indebted to him for sharing this valuable information and these priceless images with me.

Throughout this process, I have literally relived the sets, the clubs dates, and performances. James Patterson, director of the Clark University Jazz Orchestra, invited me down to his sacred basement where there was a treasure trove of material. Patterson had begun collecting, ten years prior to our meeting, material on musicians. Lloyd Terry picked me up in his red convertible and shared wonderful stories and photographs with me on the music scene as he remembered it. There are so many others who provided the same experiences. To them I am grateful.

Finally, this book was written to educate and inform the public of the major contributions that the entertainment industry had on the daily lives of African Americans in Atlanta, as well as whites who often patronized these race clubs and who were often privately and publicly entertained by these African-American entertainers in Atlanta.

As always, I want to thank and give honor to God, who has endowed me with gifts that I recognize come from Him and Him alone. To my mother, Deloris Hughes, and father, Herman "Pop" Mason Sr., I appreciate your constant words of prayer and encouragement. To sisters Dionne and Minyon and nieces and all of my family, friends, fraternity brothers, and church members, you are all indeed the wind beneath my wings. A very special thanks goes to my mentor and friend, Casper L. Jordan, who edited this and other manuscripts; Matthew Jackson, a 1996 graduate of Morehouse College who worked on the documentary aspect of this project; to my boys at "the house" who make it a joy to teach; Dr. Alton Hornsby, Mozelle Powell, and my colleagues in the History Department and the *Journal of Negro History*, who are always supportive of my endeavors; Pat Lottier and Renita Mathis of the *Atlanta Tribune*; Alexis Scott Reeves of the *Atlanta Daily World*; Earl and Carolyn Glen; the *Champion* newspaper and the *Atlanta Metro*, for your continued support of my efforts; Jo Robertson Edwards, for your sweet,

sweet spirit; Hal Lamar; A.B. Cooper; Darryl Lassiter; Mike Roberts; Ron Sailor; Lisa Leslie; and Carla Griffin.

I am also deeply indebted to the following persons for their sharing of stories, personal support, and/or loan of photographs:

Haroldeen Crowder, David Fulmer, Jondelle Johnson, Hal Lamar, Josephine Harreld Love, Stan Washington, the late B.B. Beamon, the late Griff Davis, William Coates, Edward and Betty Emory, Edwin Driskell, David Hudson, Emma Lyons Hardnett, Charles and Amarylis Hawk, Clarence Hubbard, David Hudson, Linda Jackson, Neal James, Kathyrn Jefferson, Bob Johnson, Q.P. Jones Jr., Calvin "Monk" Jones, Sarah Jones, Nancy Lawson, Clara Lowe, Ralph Mays, Bill Odum, James Patterson, Harmon Perry, Lloyd Phinazee, Marcellus Pitts, Walter "Billy" Reid, Lucille Scott, Nonye Shepherd, Lloyd Terry, Alice Washington, Lottie Heywood Watkins, Effie, Claudia, and Henry Wynn Jr., Harmon Perry, and Bill Moore for his artistic photography of the author.

Bibliography

Berry, Chuck. *Chuck Berry, the Autobiography.* New York: Simon and Schuster, 1989.

Clarke, Donald. *The Penguin Encyclopedia of Popular Music.* New York: Viking Publishers, 1989.

Cotton, Lee. *Shake Rattle and Roll: The Golden Age of American Rock 'n Roll, Volume 1: 1952–1955.* Pierian Press, 1989.

DeCurtis, Anthony, et. al. *The Rolling Stone Illustrated History of Rock and Roll.* New York: Random House, 1982.

Guralnick, Peter. *Sweet Soul Music.* New York: Harper and Row, 1986.

Handy, D. Antoinette. *Black Women in American Bands and Orchestras.* Metuchen: Scarecrow Press, 1981.

Harrison, Daphi. *Black Pearls: Blues Queens of the 1920s.* New Brunswick: Rutgers University Press.

Marsh, Dave. *The Heart of Rock and Soul: The 1,001 Greatest Singles Ever Made.* New York: Penguin Books, 1989.

Shaw, Arnold. *The World of Soul: Black Americans' Contribution to the Pop Music Scene.* New York: Cowler Book Company, 1970.

That Old Time Rock and Roll: A Chronicle of an Era 1954–1963. New York: Schirmer Books, 1989.

White, Charles. *The Life and Times of Little Richard: The Quasor.* New York: Harmony Books, 1984.

NEWSPAPERS
Atlanta Journal and Constitution, the *Atlanta Daily World* (1930–1970), the *Atlanta Independent,* the *Atlanta Inquirer,* and the *Atlanta Voice.*

About the Author: Skip Mason, a native of Atlanta, is an adjunct professor of history at Morehouse College, the founder/president of Digging It Up, Inc., and the pastor of St. James C.M.E. Church in Washington, Georgia. He is the author of several books, including *Going Against the Wind: A Pictorial History of African-Americans in Atlanta; Hidden Treasurers: Black Photographers in Atlanta; The Talented Tenth: The Seven Jewels of Alpha Phi Alpha Fraternity; African-American Life in Jacksonville; Black Atlanta in the Roaring Twenties;* and the soon-to-be-released *African-American Life in DeKalb County* and *The History of Sports in Atlanta.*